HARMONIC&MELODICMINOR JAZZGUITARSOLOING

128 Contemporary Minor Jazz Soloing Concepts For a Fresh Modern Sound

TIM**PETTINGALE**

FUNDAMENTAL**CHANGES**

Harmonic & Melodic Minor Jazz Guitar Soloing

128 Contemporary Minor Jazz Soloing Concepts For a Fresh Modern Sound

ISBN: 978-1-78933-425-8

Published by **www.fundamental-changes.com**

Copyright © 2023 Tim Pettingale

Edited by Joseph Alexander

The moral right of this author has been asserted.

All rights reserved. No part of this publication may be reproduced, stored in a retrieval system, or transmitted in any form or by any means, without the prior permission in writing from the publisher.

The publisher is not responsible for websites (or their content) that are not owned by the publisher.

www.fundamental-changes.com

For over 350 free guitar lessons with videos check out:

www.fundamental-changes.com

Join our free Facebook Community of Cool Musicians

www.facebook.com/groups/fundamentalguitar

Tag us for a share on Instagram: **FundamentalChanges**

Cover Image Copyright: Shutterstock

Contents

Introduction 5

Get the Audio 6

Chapter One – Overview of Harmonic & Melodic Minor Scales 7

Part 1 – Direct Uses of the Scales 22

Chapter Two – Chord i in the Minor ii V i 23

Chapter Three – Chord ii in the Major ii V I 27

Part 2 – Common Substitutions 31

Chapter Four – Perfect 5th Above a Dominant Chord 32

Chapter Five – Perfect 5th Above a Minor 7 Chord 40

Chapter Six – Half Step Above the V Chord 46

Chapter Seven – A Minor 3rd Above the ii Chord 51

Part 3 – More Modern Sounds 56

Chapter Eight – Harmonic Minor Over a Major 7 Chord 57

Chapter Nine – Parallel Key Melodic Minor 62

Chapter Ten – Minor 3rd Above a Dominant 7 67

Part 4 – Performance Study 72

Chapter Eleven – How to Apply These Ideas to Your Playing 73

Conclusion 88

Introduction

The Harmonic and Melodic minor scales are an area shrouded in mystery for many jazz guitar players. We know that they hold the potential for some great sounds, and that we probably *should* learn how to use them properly, but that feels like a lot of work. Learning scales is one thing, but learning where best to use them is another.

I was in the same boat as you. I could certainly hear the sonic potential of these scales, but my main problem was a lack of good resources to teach me exactly where I could use them in jazz guitar improvisation – to get the best out of them and to enrich my jazz vocabulary.

So, I set out to research how an array of modern jazz players use these scales and the substitution hacks they employ to create some really cool sounds. The result is this volume, which is an easy-to-use roadmap to integrate this sound into your playing.

I worked hard to examine all the musical possibilities of these scales in contemporary jazz and eliminated anything that sounded weird or unmusical. I also wanted to be able to explain to you how to remember and apply them in a guitaristic way.

If you're bored with your playing and feel like you often play the same kind of lines, or use the same harmonic ideas, this book is for you. It will help you to achieve the more contemporary edge to your playing you've been looking for.

I hope you enjoy it!

Tim

Get the Audio

The audio files for this book are available to download for free from **www.fundamental-changes.com**. The link is in the top right-hand corner. Click "Download Audio" and choose your instrument. Select the title of this book from the menu, and complete the form to get your audio.

We recommend that you download the files directly to your computer (not to your tablet or phone) and extract them there before adding them to your media library. If you encounter any difficulty, we provide technical support within 24 hours via the contact form.

For over 350 free guitar lessons with videos check out:

www.fundamental-changes.com

Join our free Facebook Community of Motivated Musicians

www.facebook.com/groups/fundamentalguitar

Tag us for a share on Instagram: **FundamentalChanges**

Chapter One – Overview of Harmonic & Melodic Minor Scales

In this chapter we'll start our journey by learning learn how to construct harmonic minor and melodic minor scales, and learn useful moveable patterns for them.

As I'm sure you know, there are several approaches we can take when learning scales, but when it comes to the use of the harmonic/melodic minor scales in jazz, a good starting point is to view them as overlapping box shapes based around familiar chord voicings.

This method is all about learning the scales in a way that is integral to how you'll actually use them when soloing. In this chapter, we'll work across the neck, identifying minor chord voicings, and visualize how the scale sits around each chord. Later, when we're learning licks, I'll refer to these shapes, so that you'll always understand exactly how each musical idea was formed. This will make it easier for you to create your own tasty licks later.

But first, a tiny bit of theory to aid our understanding of how these scales function.

A quick comparison of minor scales

The Harmonic Minor

The harmonic minor is almost identical to the natural minor scale, apart from one note: its 7th degree is raised a half step. But that one note makes all the difference. It transforms the very *inside* sounding natural minor into something hauntingly exotic. The harmonic minor has been used widely in jazz, but also has applications in neo-classical rock, metal and surf rock. Set your guitar to the bridge pickup, crank up the splashy spring reverb and think spaghetti western. Or listen to the Rolling Stones *Paint it Black,* to capture the broad potential of this scale.

In jazz, its natural home is the minor ii V i chord progression. For example, we can play A Harmonic Minor over chord i (Am7) in the sequence Bm7b5 – E7#9 – Am7.

But as we'll see, there are many other places where this scale can be used to great effect in both minor and major contexts. We'll get to that in due course, but first let's compare the notes of A Harmonic Minor to the A Natural Minor scale.

A Natural Minor	A	B	C	D	E	F	G
A Harmonic Minor	A	B	C	D	E	F	G#

Notice the raised 7th degree of A Harmonic Minor (G# instead of G).

The Melodic Minor

In classical harmony, the melodic minor takes one form when ascending and a different form when descending. The ascending form contains the "altered notes" when compared to the natural minor, while the descending form mirrors it exactly. Over time, however, jazz musicians have done away with this technicality and tend to use the *ascending form* for all purposes.

The melodic minor sits comfortably in the major ii V I, where we might play A Melodic Minor over chord ii (Am7) in the sequence Am7 – D7 – Gmaj7.

But like the harmonic minor, it can be used in many more contexts, and once you've learned the scale patterns, you'll be able to throw away the rule book and use your ears as we explore together all the places it can be applied to great effect in modern jazz.

The melodic minor scale has two notes that are different from the natural minor, and one note different from the harmonic minor. Take a moment to compare all three minor scales in the table below.

A Natural Minor	A	B	C	D	E	F	G
A Harmonic Minor	A	B	C	D	E	F	G#
A Melodic Minor	A	B	C	D	E	**F#**	**G#**

The melodic minor has both raised 6th and 7th degrees (F# and G#) compared to the natural minor, and just the 6th degree is different if we compare it to the harmonic minor.

Two scales - a wealth of musical applications

My discovery of using harmonic and melodic minor scales in a practical way, when soloing over jazz standards, is that in a few musical situations, either one will work just fine. But in many other contexts, one scale often works much more beautifully than the other. The aim of this book is to guide you regarding where to use each scale to get the best out of it *and* create the most melodically interesting and pleasing jazz lines.

We'll begin by learning the harmonic minor scale across the neck.

Five minor chord voicings

If you were comping over an A minor chord vamp and wanted to keep things interesting, rather than playing in just one region of the neck, a good approach would be to mix and match these five, closely connected voicings:

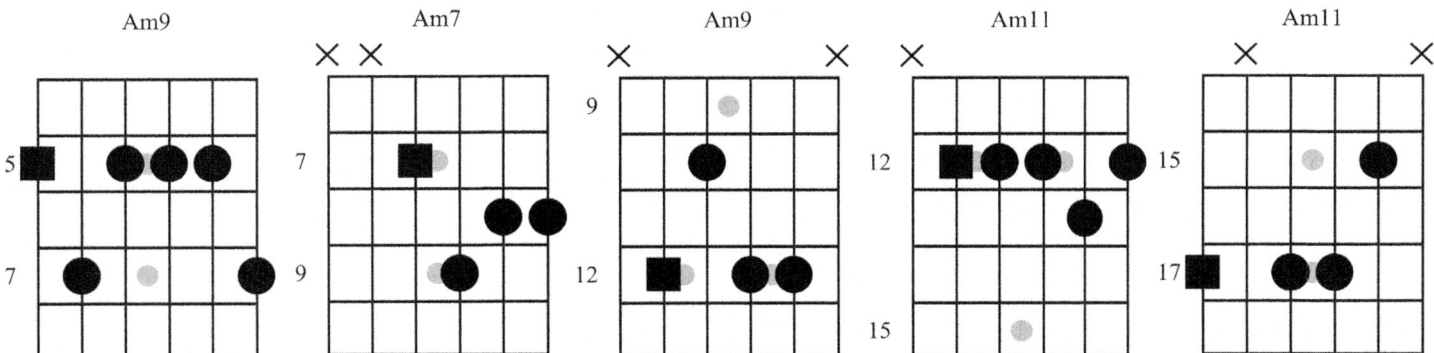

This way of organizing chords into five shapes across the neck is similar to the CAGED system, but we're using specific jazz chord voicings – chords that you're likely to want to play over a jazz standard.

Based around these five shapes we'll build five patterns for *both* scales, starting with the harmonic minor, then repeating the process for the melodic minor.

From left to right, we'll refer to the chords above as Shape 1, Shape 2 etc. The examples that follow are in the key of A Minor, so when we get to Shape 5, rather than learn the scale up at the 15th-17th frets (tricky on an archtop), we'll move it down to the 3rd-5th frets:

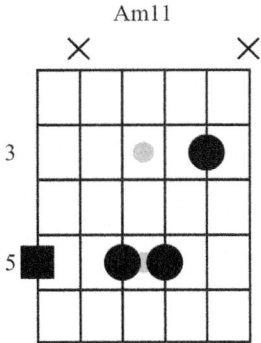

Harmonic minor – five scale shapes

Let's look at how the notes of the harmonic minor fit around each shape and practice the scale patterns. We're not going to spend lots of time on scale drills here, because I want you to be able to play some useful licks as quickly as possible – but spend as much time as you can familiarizing yourself with these shapes. It would be ideal to make them a part of your warm-up routine.

Shape 1

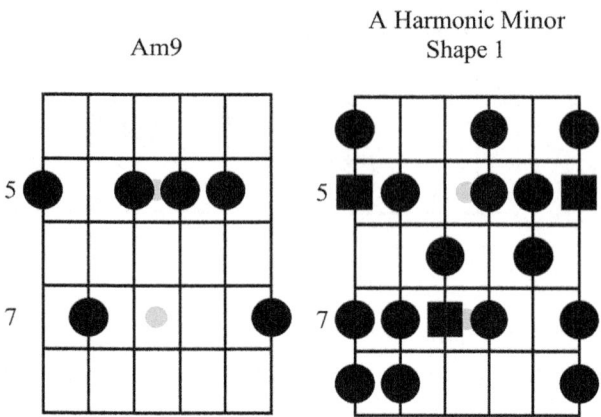

Take a moment to visualize the chord shape above and think about how the harmonic minor scale is arranged around it. The key characteristic of the harmonic minor is immediately apparent: because of its raised 7th degree, there is always a note a half step below the root note (G# to A).

When we begin soloing with this scale, that half step movement will sound like a chromatic approach note to begin with, even though it belongs to the scale. The positioning of this note, and the scale pattern it naturally creates, is the key to some cool harmonic minor licks you'll have heard played by Joe Pass, Pat Martino, Wes Montgomery, Pat Metheny and more.

Play the chord, then play the scale ascending and descending. Practice it several times because it's vital to begin to build the chord-scale relationship – both in the muscle memory of your fingers and also in your ears – as you listen to how the intervals work over the chord.

Example 1a

Now play Shape 2 and the harmonic minor scale pattern built around it. To keep us focused on where the root note is, we'll play the scale from the root on the fourth string then ascend. Then we'll descend all the way down to the sixth string and back up to the root. Take a few moments to visualize the chord shape and the notes positioned around it before playing the exercise.

Shape 2

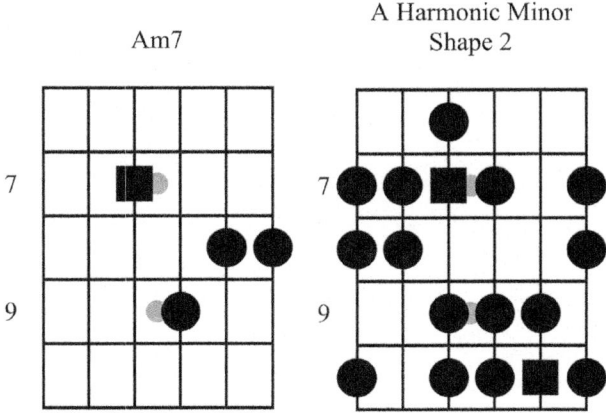

Example 1b

Here's Shape 3, built around an Am9 voicing with the root note on the fifth string, 12th fret. Play from the root and ascend the scale, then descend all the way down to the sixth string and back up to the root.

Shape 3

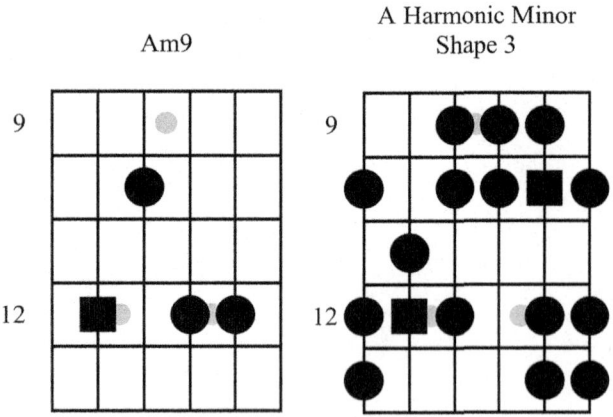

Example 1c

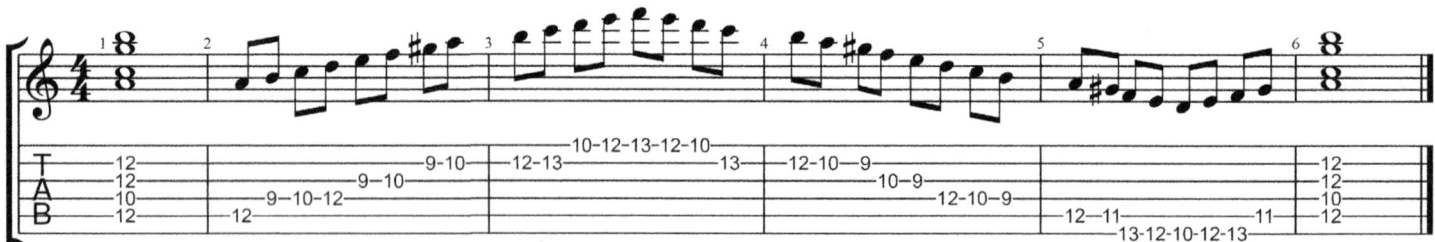

Shape 4 is based around this Am11 voicing at the 12th fret. The minor 11 chord is essential when playing modal tunes like *So What* or *Footprints*, but you can also use it in ii V I sequences for a more modern sound. Play the chord, then play the scale ascending from the 5th string root, then descending to the sixth string and back up to the root.

Shape 4

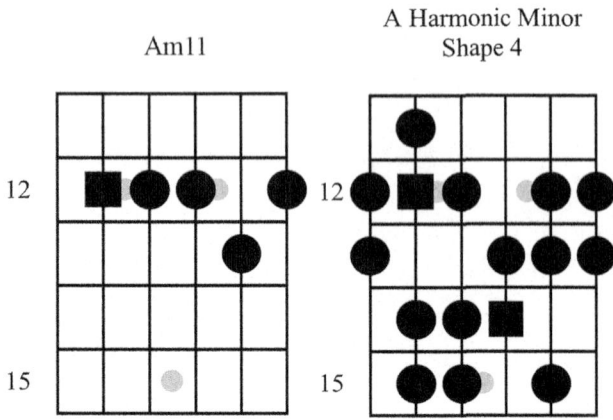

Example 1d

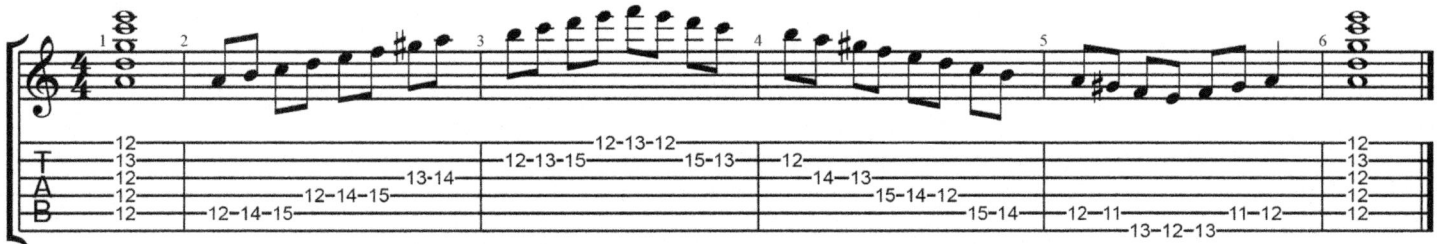

Shape 5

Shape 5 is a little more spread out than previous shapes. To make it easily playable, it is arranged over six frets rather than five. Approach it by playing the sixth string root note with the fourth finger, with the first finger resting at the 2nd fret.

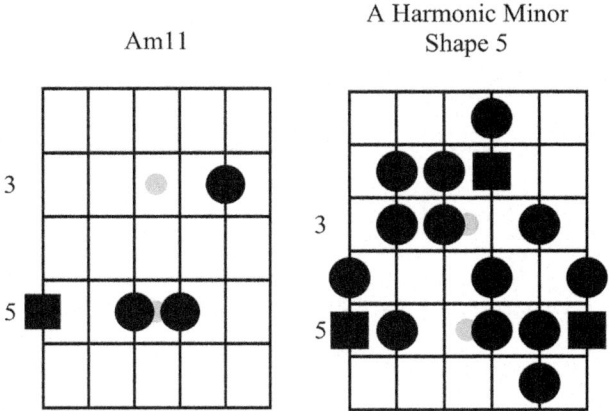

Example 1e

Test the scale over a one-chord vamp

There are lots of great jazz standards built around just a few chords. The modal vamps of Miles Davis and John Coltrane (*So What* and *Impressions*), use just two minor chords that modulate back and forth a half step. Wayne Shorter's minor modal blues *Footprints* has long periods of playing over just one chord, and Herbie Hancock's *Canteloupe Island* uses a three-chord cycle with numerous consecutive bars of Fm7.

These tunes are ideal for practicing harmonic and melodic minor scales over, because you can really hear the effect of the intervals at work. Let's test the sound of the harmonic minor now over a static A minor vamp. The five licks that follow are based around the five scale shapes in order.

First, here is the classic harmonic minor lick you'll have heard played often, using Shape 1. The notes on the first string almost sound like an enclosure, but of course they're all scale tones. Those four simple notes evoke the melancholy sound of the scale.

Example 1f

In Shape 2, we have notes at the 9th and 10th fret on three adjacent strings, so it makes sense to make a feature of them, as in bar four here.

Example 1g

Using Shape 3, here's a descending phrase. The motif almost begins to repeat in bar two, but then we head in a different direction.

Example 1h

Here's an improvised line played with Shape 4. How we sequence the notes in a phrase has a great bearing on the kind of vibe we conjure up and this line, quite by accident, has hints of a Bach melodic variation.

Example 1i

Finally, a line based around Shape 5. We can mix and match rhythms to play more creative lines and this idea combines 1/8th notes with longer held notes and 1/8th note triplets.

Example 1j

Melodic minor – five scale shapes

Now we'll repeat this process for the melodic minor scale. We'll use the same five minor chord voicings as our starting point. We'll visualize how the melodic minor scale fits around these chord shapes, then practice the scale. Then we'll test it over the same A minor vamp as before and note the differences in sound.

Although it's tempting to think, "All I have to do is take the A Harmonic Minor shape and raise its F note to F#", in fact, that small change results in some quite different arrangements on the fretboard, if we want the scale to be easily playable around the chord shape.

Take a look at melodic minor Shape 1 below. Play the chord, then the scale, and listen to the intervals it creates.

The melodic minor shares the G# note of the harmonic minor, so it has that "chromatic approach note" sound going on when we begin to play lines with it. But its unique F# note is what yields its distinctive flavor. F# is the note you'd add to an A minor chord if you wanted to make it an Am6. This note means that where the harmonic minor sounds tense and exotic, the melodic minor sounds cool and sophisticated.

Shape 1

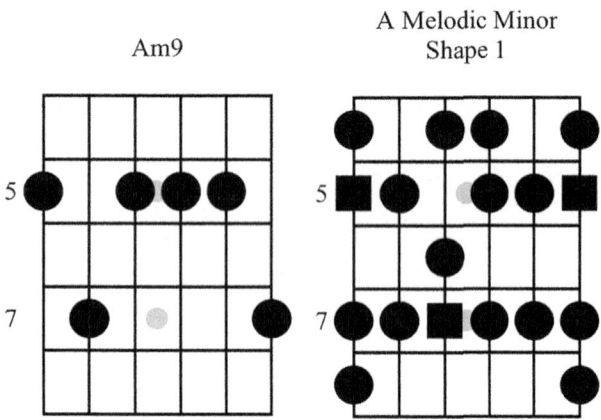

Example 1k

Now play Shape 2 of A Melodic Minor, beginning on the fourth string root, ascending. Descend down to the sixth string, then all the way back up to the root note. This is one of my favorite shapes for melodic minor because it really brings out those cool tones.

Shape 2

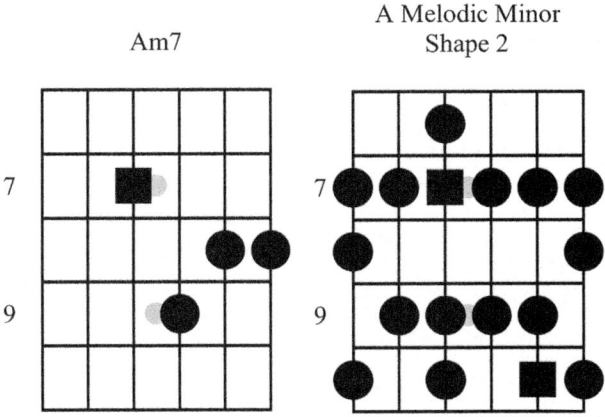

Example 11

Next, we move on to Shape 3, based around the Am9 chord at the 12th fret.

Shape 3

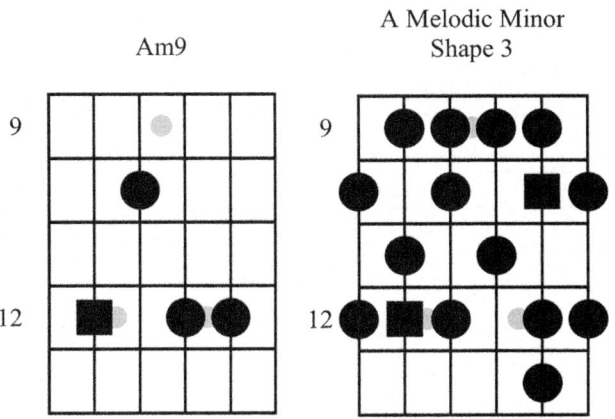

Example 1m

Here's Shape 4, played ascending from its fifth string root.

Shape 4

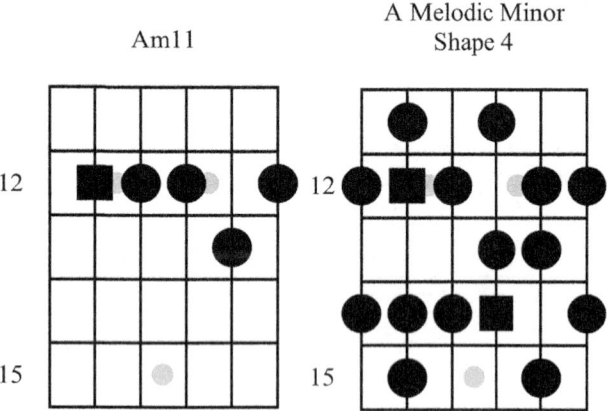

Example 1n

And, finally, Shape 5, which we'll learn in the middle register.

Shape 5

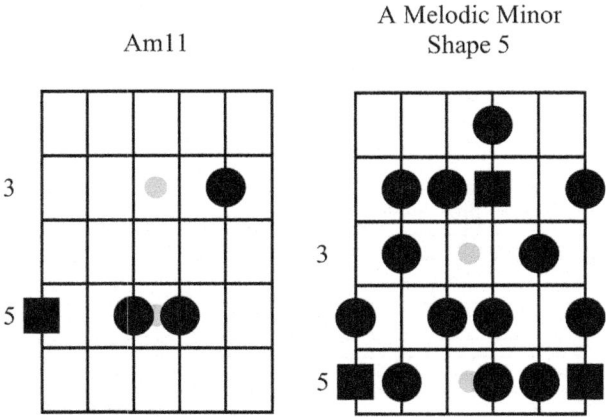

Example 1o

Test the scale over a one-chord vamp

Just as we did for the harmonic minor, we'll now apply each of the five scale shapes and test the melodic minor scale over a one-chord vamp in A Minor. Listen out for the difference this scale brings to the music and think about how it compares to the harmonic minor.

Listen out for the melodic minor's unique F# note in this first line using Shape 1. The scale still has that melancholy feeling, but somehow a cooler edge too.

Example 1p

This line using Shape 2 focuses on the middle part of the shape where there are notes on the 7th and 9th frets on consecutive strings. It gives the line a kind of pentatonic sound, but then in bar three the G# and F# color tones of the scale are emphasized.

Example 1q

Here's a reminder that the classic harmonic minor lick also exists within the melodic minor. We open with that phrase, using Shape 3 as the basis of the line. This phrase weaves around the color notes of the scale. Look out for the timing in bar three where the triplet phrase begins on the & of beat 2.

Example 1r

The next example uses Shape 4. This line also makes a feature of the F# note, hitting it on beat 1 of bar four and holding it for the duration. Over an A minor harmony, it makes the sound of an Am6 chord.

Example 1s

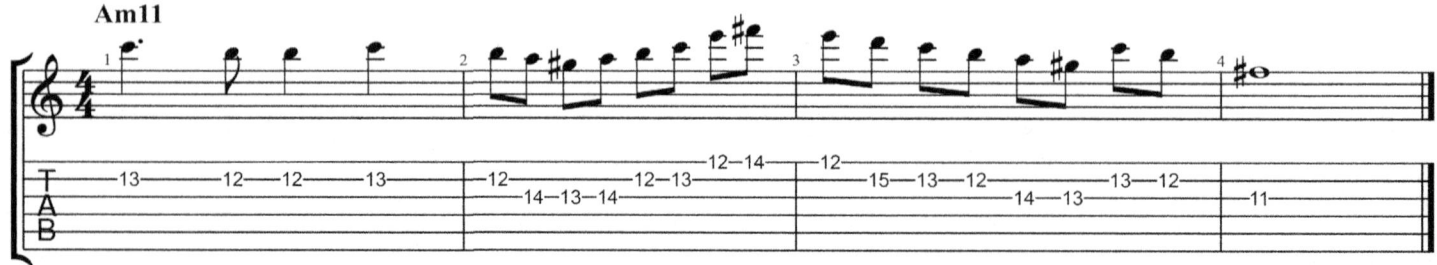

The melodic minor always sounds darker than the harmonic minor to me and here's an idea that brings out that aspect of the scale. It has a simple repeating four-note motif that descends through the Shape 5 pattern. This time we end on a strong G# note, which implies the sound of an Am(Maj7) chord.

Example 1t

So far, for each scale we've learned the five shapes that enable us to cover the range of the fretboard, and we've road tested each one over a static minor chord. Return to this chapter as often as you can in your practice times to make sure you've thoroughly learned the scale patterns and can visualize them fitting around the reference chords.

In the next section of the book, we'll look at how to apply both scales in the context of the ubiquitous ii V I progression. We'll also begin to look at phrasing ideas that move between shapes, rather than staying in one zone (which is why it's really important to know those shapes!)

Part 1 – Direct Uses of the Scales

In the rest of this book, we'll look the most useful places we can use the harmonic and melodic scales in jazz. Later, we'll explore how to use substitution ideas to create jazz licks that contain sophisticated tensions, but first let's get to grips with the simplest and most direct use of these scales: over minor chords in ii V I progressions.

First, we'll look at how to use the harmonic minor scale in a *minor* ii V i, then we'll move onto the melodic minor in a *major* II V I.

Chapter Two – Chord i in the Minor ii V i

The natural home of the harmonic minor scale is the minor ii V i progression. On any jazz standard chord chart, if you see the sequence Bm7b5 – E7#9 – Am9, the A Harmonic Minor scale will be a great choice.

But it's not just for the A minor chord. We can actually use A Harmonic Minor to solo over *every* chord in that sequence. Let's briefly look at why this is the case.

If we take the notes of the A Harmonic Minor scale and harmonize them into chords by stacking intervals in 3rds, it results in the following set of 7th chords:

A	B	C	D	E	F	G#
Am(Maj7)	Bm7b5	Cmaj7#5	Dm7	E7	Fmaj7	G#dim7
A C E G#	B D F A	C E G# B	D F A C	E G# B D	F A C E	G# B D F

Notice that Bm7b5 (chord ii) and E7 (chord V) naturally occur in the scale.

Technically, chord i in a minor ii V i should be Amin(Maj7), but it has a dissonant, unresolved sound, so 99% of the time jazz musicians will play a straight A minor or Am7 instead.

Because the harmonic minor scale fits every chord in the minor ii V i sequence, this gives us melodic options. We can choose to spell out the ii and V chords with arpeggios and save the harmonic minor scale licks for the i chord, or we can apply the scale over the entire sequence. We'll explore both ideas in the lines that follow.

To build jazz lines over the minor ii V i, we'll use the scale shapes we learned in the previous chapter. This should further reinforce the patterns for you and enable you to see how they work in practice.

First, here are two lines using A Harmonic Minor Shape 1.

These two examples use arpeggio ideas for the ii and V chords and the harmonic minor scale on chord i.

Example 2a

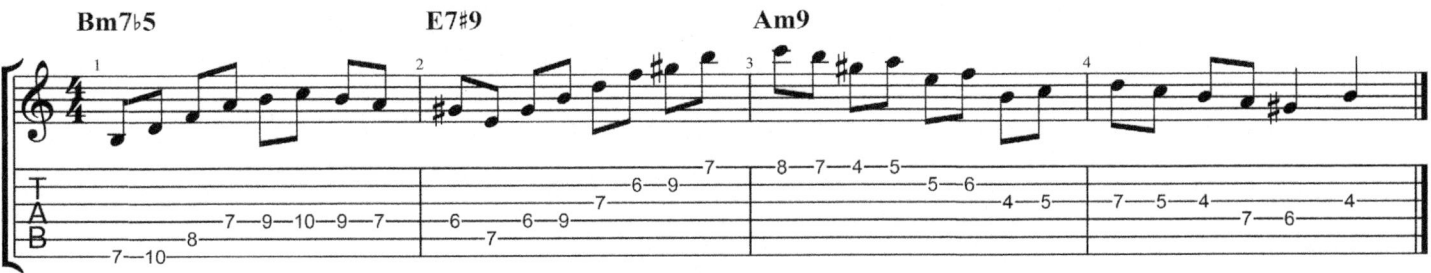

This line descends Bm7b5 arpeggio notes, ascends E7#9 and uses a half step movement to get into Shape 1 of A Harmonic Minor.

Example 2b

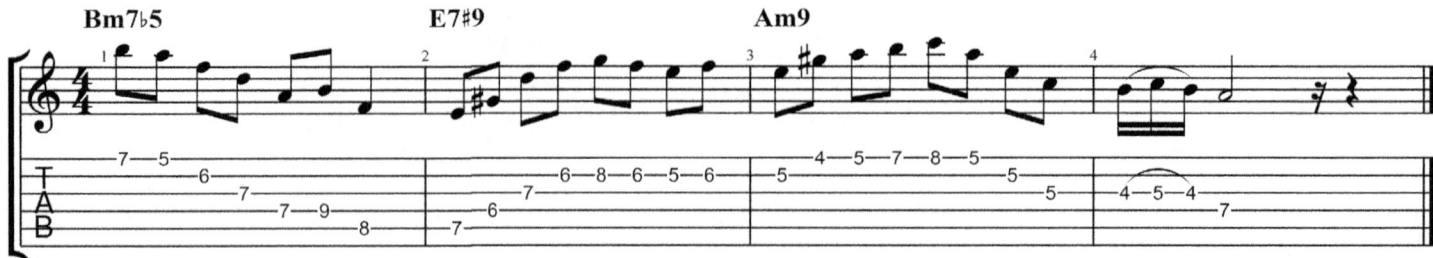

Now we move on to two lines that use Shape 2 of the scale. Again, these two licks focus on arpeggio tones throughout bars 1-2 and save the harmonic minor scale for the i chord.

Starting with a Bm7b5 ascending arpeggio in 2nd position, this lick transitions up into Shape 2. Notice that we're playing the Shape 2 pattern from the E note on the fifth string, straight to the top.

Example 2c

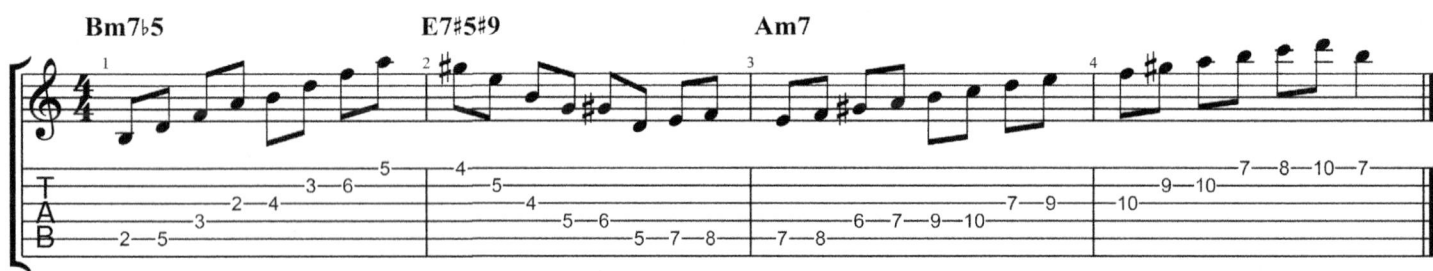

The next idea is organized into 1/8th note triplets and utilizes Shape 2 on the middle strings.

Example 2d

The remaining licks in this chapter use the harmonic minor scale over the *whole* ii V i progression. Here, we are less concerned with spelling out the sound of the ii and V chords with arpeggios, and more interested in what the scale has to offer.

Each of these lines weaves around the scale tones in its respective shape, so I won't give you a detailed breakdown of the ideas. Instead, as you learn each line, think about the pathways through the scale shape that you like the sound of and commit them to memory.

These two lines come from Shape 3.

Example 2e

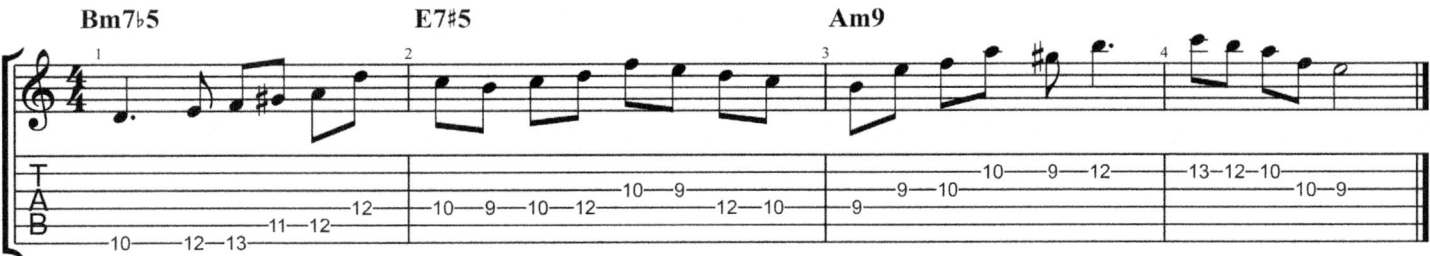

Example 2f

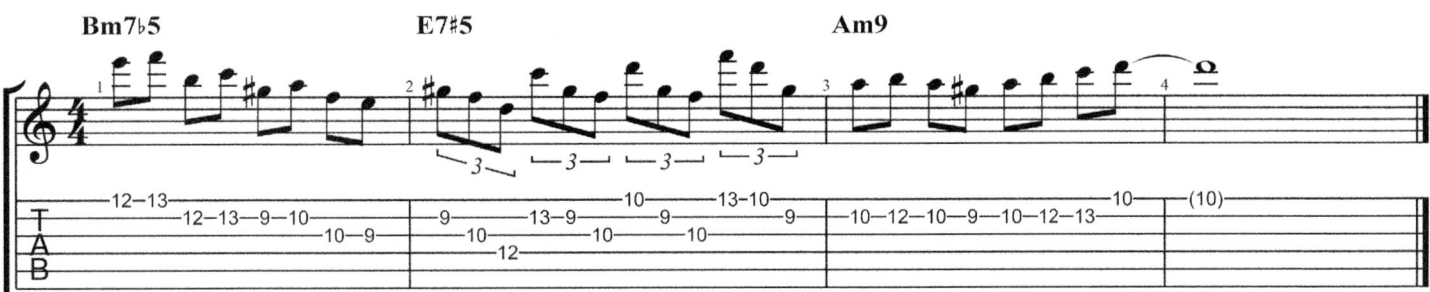

Now we move onto Shape 4.

Example 2g

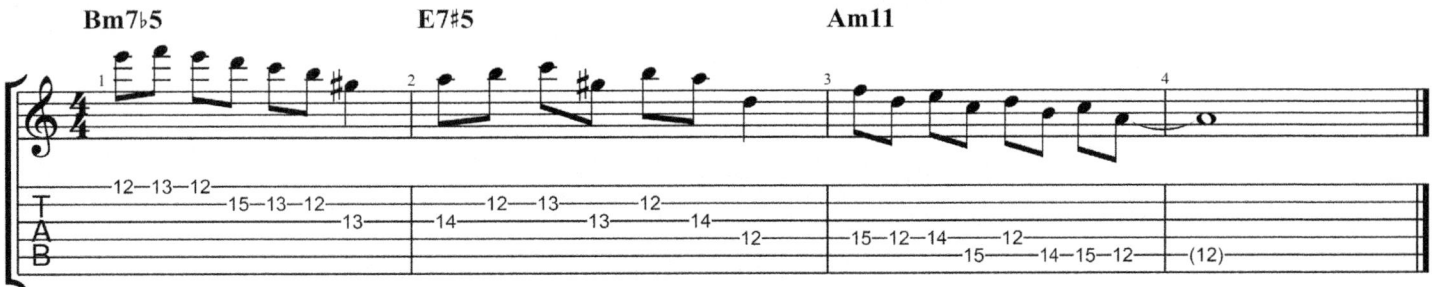

Example 2h

And, lastly, two lines from Shape 5.

Example 2i

Example 2j

We've had a taste of the potential of the harmonic minor scale in its minor ii V i context. In the next chapter we'll see how the melodic minor functions in the major ii V I.

Chapter Three – Chord ii in the Major ii V I

When it comes to the major ii V I, trial, error, and experience have taught me that the melodic minor sounds best as the scale of choice. It can be used very effectively over the ii chord, but for reasons similar to the harmonic minor, we can play it over the whole ii V if we exercise a bit of taste and discretion.

If you see this progression written on a chart: Am7 – D7 – Gmaj7, you can use the A Melodic Minor scale to play over the whole sequence.

If we examine the notes in the individual chords, we find that the A Melodic Minor scale contains three of the four notes in Am7, all four notes of D7, and three of the four notes in Gmaj7.

The elephant in the room is the fact that A Melodic Minor has a G# note, while the chords Am7 and Gmaj7 both contain the note G!

But this is not an insurmountable problem. When we play licks, we just treat that G# as we would a chromatic approach note, then resolve it to different scale tones. In fact, it can serve to add some satisfying tension to our lines. Don't think of this as an "avoid note" lesson, think of it as a lesson in ear training!

Let's play some lines that use this sound, based around the five melodic minor scales shapes illustrated in Chapter One. However, so that we can begin to build more expansive ideas, for the first time we'll break out of single shape patterns and combine two adjacent scale shapes. Learning to move between shapes will really open up the fretboard for you and give you lots more options when composing licks.

We'll do this gradually though, so that you can visualize the shapes and how we can move between them. We'll also mix and match some arpeggio ideas with pure melodic minor scale licks.

Example 3a uses just Shape 1 of A Melodic Minor.

This first example ascends straight up Shape 1 in bar one, before becoming more selective with the note choices. The whole line is scale focused, rather than thinking in terms of arpeggios.

Example 3a

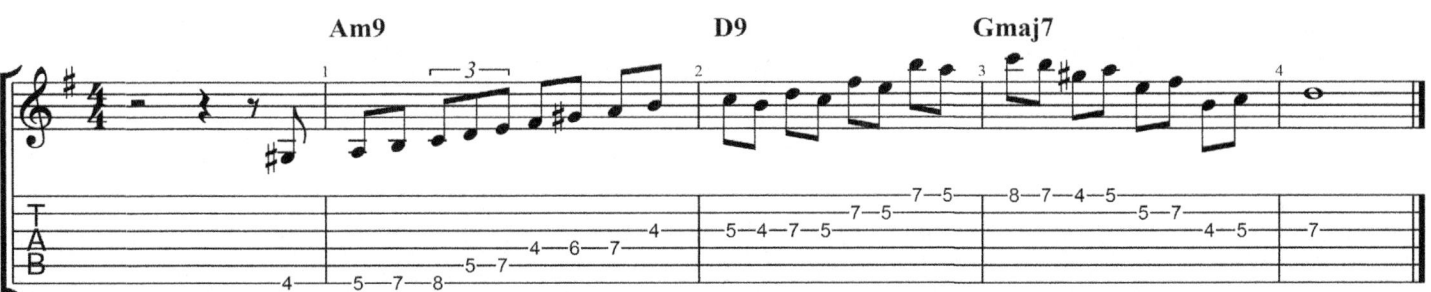

This idea uses Shape 2 of A Melodic Minor. In bar three we avoid playing the G# note over Gmaj7 and select the notes to form a pentatonic sounding phrase. The G# is allowed to feature in bar four as an approach note.

Example 3b

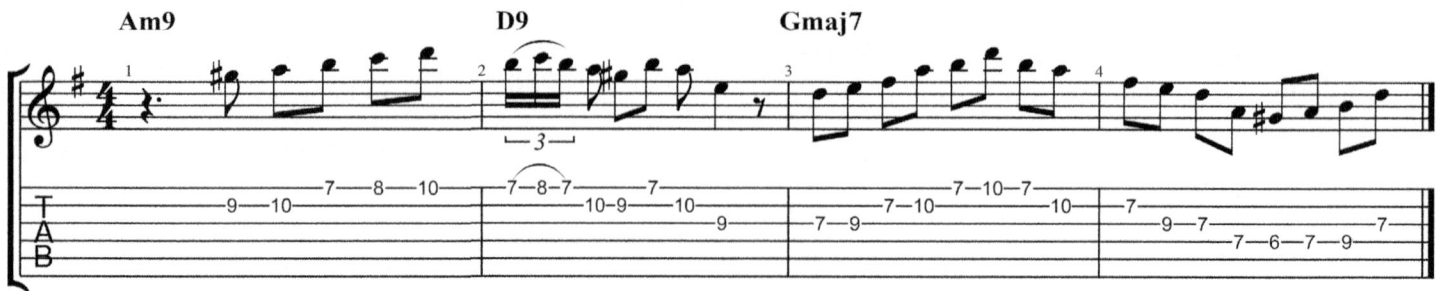

For the next line, we'll combine shapes 1 and 2, so we can play across a greater range of the neck.

We begin in Shape 1 and use notes on the fourth string to transition into Shape 2. (Compare the shapes and you'll see that the notes on the 6th/7th frets of the fourth string overlap). The pathway this creates allows us to move from 5th to 10th position, and the line ends with a Gmaj7 arpeggio phrase.

Example 3c

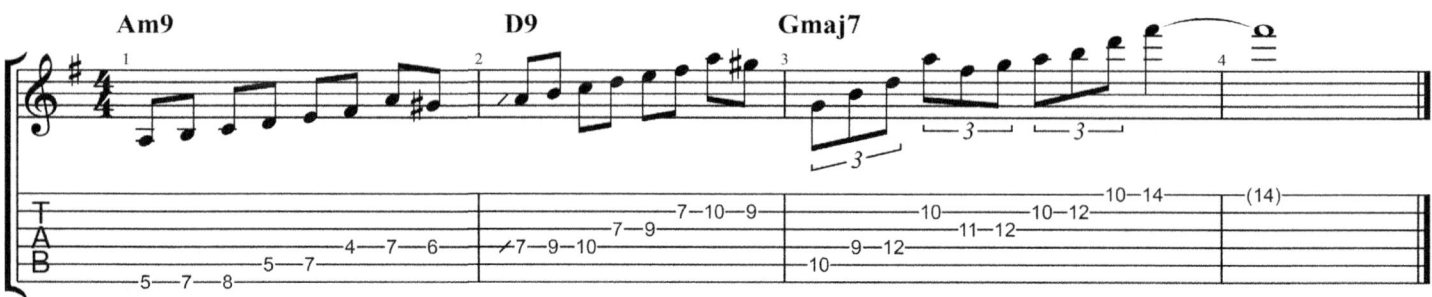

We're going to continue this process by playing a line that uses just Shape 3, then the subsequent example will combine shapes 2 and 3.

Example 3d

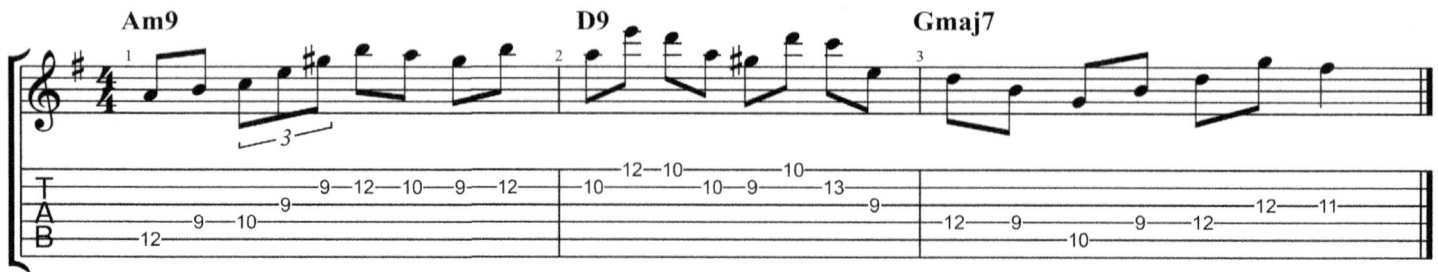

This line uses descending notes on the top string to transition from Shape 3 into Shape 2. It also has a repetitive phrasing idea to create a short motif.

Example 3e

The next example is built around Shape 4 of the scale. In most of these examples, we're playing A Melodic Minor over the Am and D7 chords, then we bring out the sound of the Gmaj7 with arpeggio figures or G Major scale notes.

Example 3f

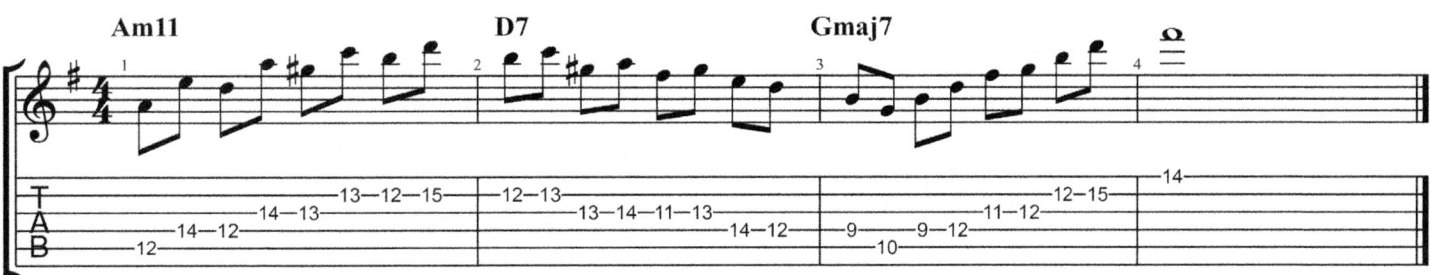

Now let's combine Shape 3 and Shape 4. This line uses the notes on the fifth string to transition from Shape 3 up into Shape 4.

Example 3g

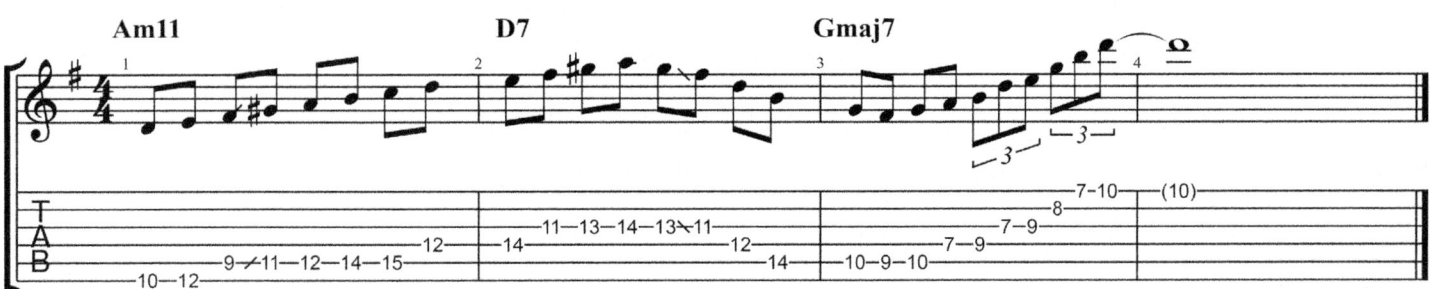

Now let's play a line based around Shape 5.

Example 3h

Shape 5 and Shape 1 dovetail together, so let's complete our process of combining adjacent shapes with a line that spans them. This is a more challenging line that has a 1/16th note run that requires some slide-shifting position changes.

Example 3i

To end this chapter, let's play a line that combines shapes 1, 2 and 3. A motif played on the top two strings glues the line together as it ascends through the shapes.

Example 3j

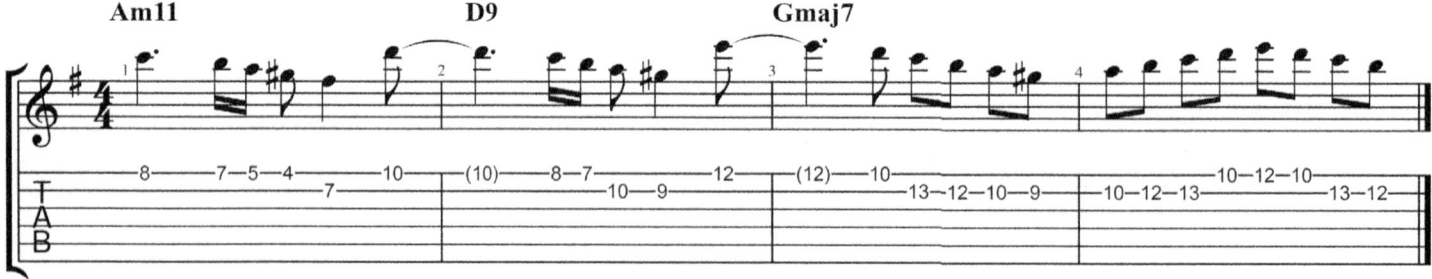

In this chapter we've begun to get used to the darker colors of the melodic minor and used it in the major ii V I progression. You'll have seen that we need to be a little careful when using it over the I chord, but we can allow our ears to guide us and be the judge of which tensions are pleasing and which are not!

Part 2 – Common Substitutions

We've seen that the harmonic and melodic minor scales add a touch of sophistication to our jazz lines when used in a simple, direct manner, but they can really help raise our game when it comes to creating interesting melodic lines if we introduce some simple substitution ideas.

In the next four chapters we'll look at the substitution ideas that have formed part of the vocabulary of players such as Pat Martino, Pat Metheny, Joe Pass, Jim Hall and Wes Montgomery. Once you've learned your harmonic/melodic minor scales and know them pretty well, these easily memorized hacks are great to apply the knowledge you've gained in a new way, and they will open up new harmonic territory for you to explore.

Chapter Four – Perfect 5th Above a Dominant Chord

The first substitution idea is one that both Wes Montgomery and Pat Martino used extensively, and also features in Pat Metheny's vocabulary. When we encounter a dominant 7 chord, we can play a minor scale whose root is a perfect 5th above the root of the dominant chord.

Let's say the dominant chord is D7. A perfect 5th above the note D is A. So, over the D7 chord we can play A minor-based scalic ideas – in this instance, using the *melodic* minor scale.

Why it works

Here's a reminder of the notes of A Melodic Minor: A, B, C, D, E, F#, G#

The chord tones of D7 are D, F#, A, C.

The A Melodic Minor scale contains all the chord tones of D7, then adds 13th (B), 9th (E), and #11 (G#) tensions.

The combination of inside and extended tones, plus that one altered tone, makes this a very useful idea and it immediately adds a more sophisticated edge to our jazz vocabulary. Using it makes us sound like we're really nailing the harmony, because we're playing every chord tone plus some carefully chosen cool notes!

There are three places where we can use this idea in jazz, and you've already inadvertently used one of them.

1. Over the V chord in a ii V I

In the previous chapter we played over the sequence Am7 – D7 – Gmaj7. Here, our focus was mostly the ii chord (Am7), but we established that we could, in fact, play A Melodic Minor over the whole sequence. When we played A Melodic Minor ideas over the D7 chord, we were effectively using the "minor a perfect 5th above a dominant chord" substitution.

So, we've covered the idea of using this substitution in the context of the ii V I, but there are two more musical situations in which this idea flourishes – and these will be the focus of this chapter.

2. Over a static dominant chord vamp

If you've been used to playing standards like *Blue Bossa* and *Autumn Leaves*, it can be a bit of a curve ball when someone hands you a chart for *Maiden Voyage* by Herbie Hancock or *Bolivia* by Cedar Walton, both of which have long passages of static dominant chords. Knowing that you can play a melodic minor scale a 5th above the root of those dominant chords is an absolute jam session life-saver.

3. On every chord in a blues

A simple blues is made up of three dominant chords. You can use this substitution idea to play a *different* melodic minor scale on every chord in the blues.

Let's take a blues in G, for example. I'm sure you can quickly work this out for yourself, but here are the relevant melodic minor scale substitutions we can use:

Chord I = G7 (Play D Melodic Minor scale)

Chord IV = C7 (Play G Melodic Minor scale)

Chord V = D7 (Play A Melodic Minor scale)

This concept introduces a lot of melodic territory for us to explore. We can focus on just one substitution and mix it with pentatonic and blues-based ideas, or we can go wholesale down the melodic minor route and play substitutions on every chord.

If you've ever been frustrated by the fact that you tend to play the same licks when soloing over a jazz-blues, here's your answer! Introduce some melodic minor substitutions into your vocabulary and you'll instantly elevate your solos.

First, however, let's look at a few ideas that use this substitution idea over multiple bars of a static dominant chord. So far, all the ideas we've looked at have used A minor scalic ideas, so to keep us on our toes we'll change key.

In the first three examples we're playing over a Bb7 chord. There are lots of jazz standards and blues in this key because they were written on/for the tenor saxophone, which is a Bb instrument.

Find a perfect 5th interval above Bb on your guitar and you'll see that we need to play the F Melodic Minor scale. We therefore need to transpose the melodic minor scale shapes we've learned from A to F to accommodate the key change. Don't worry though, I've included those shapes below.

When you have time, check out the tune *Freedom Jazz Dance* by Eddie Harris from his 1965 album *The In Sound*. This modal tune is based on just one chord (Bb7), yet it works amazingly well and has a killer groove! (As a sidebar, this album has a fantastic lineup of personnel that includes Cedar Walton on piano, Ron Carter on bass and Billy Higgins on drums). This tune's popularity was cemented when Miles Davis covered it on his *Miles Smiles* album.

Here are all five shapes of F Melodic Minor for reference. I've ordered them low-to-high, in order of their position on the fretboard.

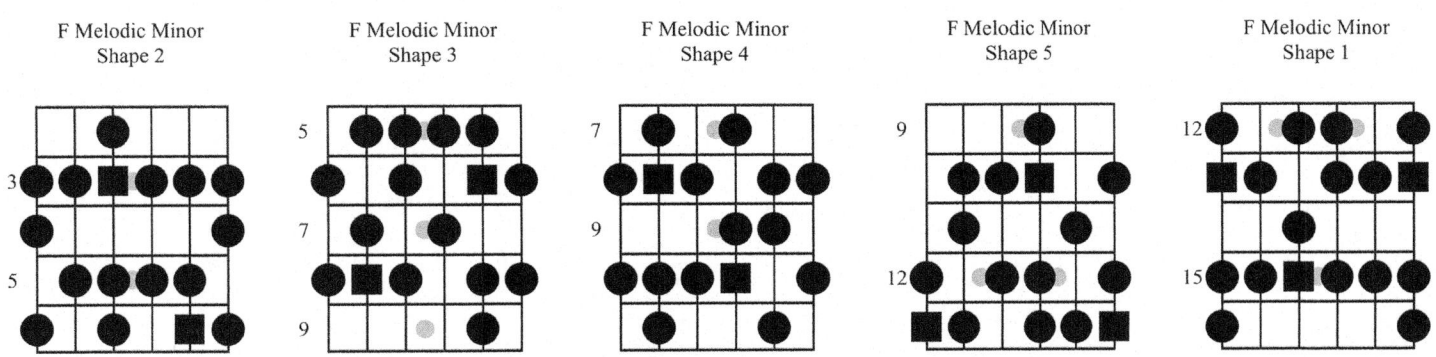

This first example begins in Shape 3 of F Melodic Minor. I deliberately chose to start here so that we could begin the line with a Bb bass note. The line transitions from Shape 3 into Shape 4 and we end on an F note, the 5th of the underlying Bb7 chord.

I'm sure you'll immediately see how effective this idea can be. The note choices it opens up sound sophisticated and help us to avoid the bluesy clichés we might otherwise be tempted to play.

Example 4a

Example 4b uses Shape 4 for bars 1-2 and jumps into Shape 5 for bars 3-4. The line begins on the F root note of the melodic minor scale, which over Bb7 is like launching from its 5th. The lick ends on a dissonant sounding E note this time, the b5 of Bb7.

Example 4b

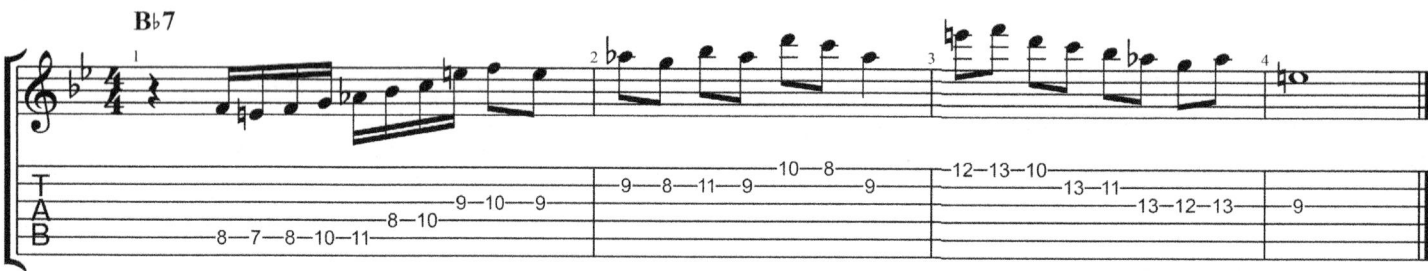

The next lines uses Shape 2 and plays a sequenced four-note descending pattern. This lick ends on a C note, which is the 9th of Bb7.

Example 4c

The previous three lines have given a taste of the kind of ideas we can play over static dominant chords in modal jazz tunes. I'm sure you'll appreciate already how different this sounds to taking a pentatonic or mixolydian approach.

Now let's open up the idea further and see how we can apply it in the context of a blues, over three different dominant chords.

We'll change key again, this time to G Major. When you come to explore these ideas on your own, try jamming over the changes to the Miles Davis tune *All Blues*.

Here, we're going break down the blues into four-bar chunks and play a couple of ideas for each four-bar section, applying the relevant melodic minor scale, before moving onto the next section.

First, we have four bars of G7, so we'll be using the D Melodic Minor scale. I've given you the shapes for D Melodic Minor below, but for the other two dominant chords in the progression I want you to transpose them for yourself.

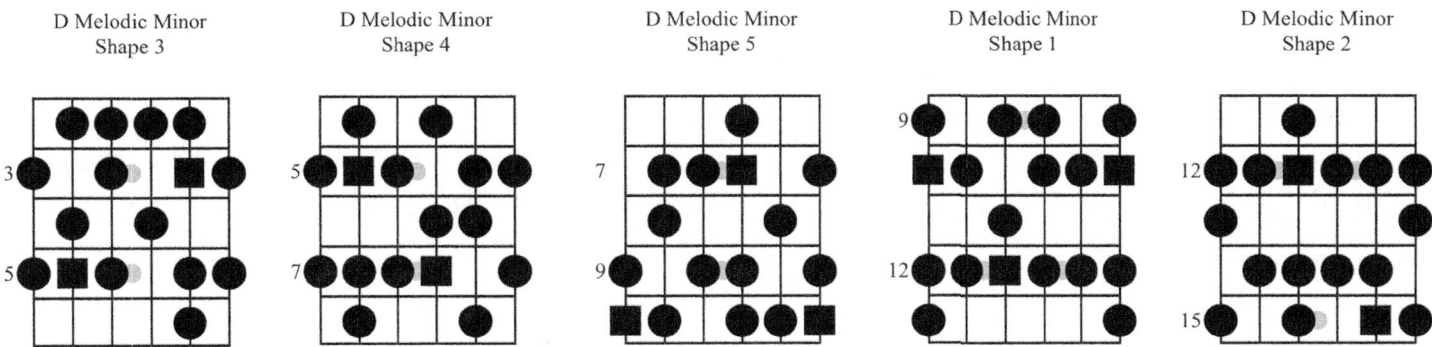

In these examples, we will combine the melodic minor scale with some bluesy ideas, so that you get a feel for how to incorporate the melodic minor sound into your playing in a natural, unforced way. If I was improvising over this sequence without thinking, I'd probably include the occasional chromatic passing note, so we'll do that too, but I'll point out to you when it occurs.

In this example, we start with a bluesy phrase followed by an ascending line in Shape 4 of D Melodic Minor. The opening phrase is echoed in bar three, then we have a Shape 4 descending lick.

I used one passing note on the second string, 7th fret, in bar four to keep the 1/16th note momentum going.

Example 4d

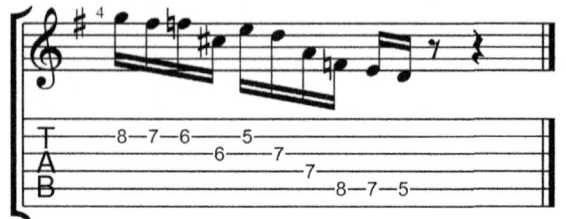

In contrast, here's a line that uses D Melodic Minor throughout. It also moves through every scale shape, transitioning on different strings, to cover the full range of the fretboard. An idea like this shows the sonic potential of the melodic minor to produce some very contemporary sounds.

Example 4e

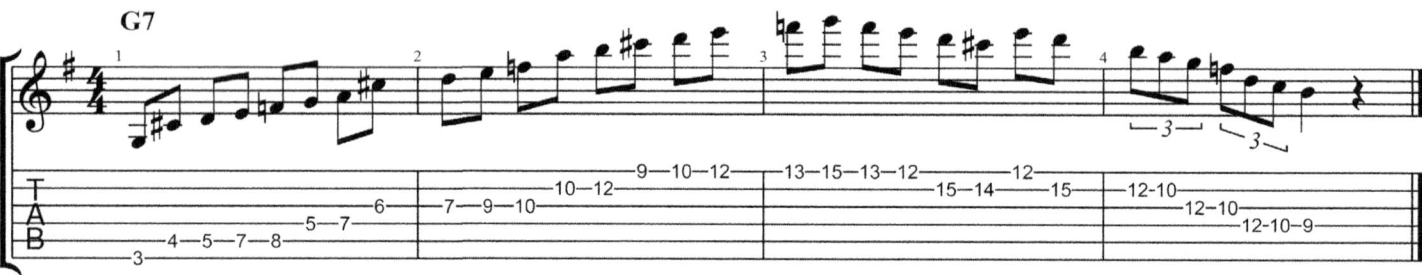

We've looked at two contrasting ideas we can use to solo over the first four bars of a blues in G. Next, a couple of ideas to play over the IV chord (C7), transitioning back to the I chord.

A perfect 5th above C is the note G, so over the C7 chord we'll play the G Melodic Minor scale. When we return to the G7 chord, we'll revert to D Melodic Minor.

I won't spell out the shapes for G Melodic Minor this time, as it's good for you to begin to work out how to transpose them for yourself (hint: in this instance, you can just refer to the A Melodic Minor shapes and visualize them all shifted down a whole step).

The main challenge here is quickly switching from one melodic minor scale to the next and doing so in a musically pleasing way over the changes. I won't deny it, refining this skill is a lifetime's work and none of us have arrived yet – but we're here to learn together!

The easiest way to approach this is to compare adjacent shapes for the scales and look for likely transition points along the strings.

Bar three features an idea we've not yet explored (though we'll do so in later chapters), which is to pick out triad patterns that exist within the melodic minor scale. Refer to the D Melodic Minor shapes shown earlier, and you'll see that I'm picking out three-note patterns on the top three strings, descending from Shape 5, through Shape 4, into Shape 3.

Example 4f

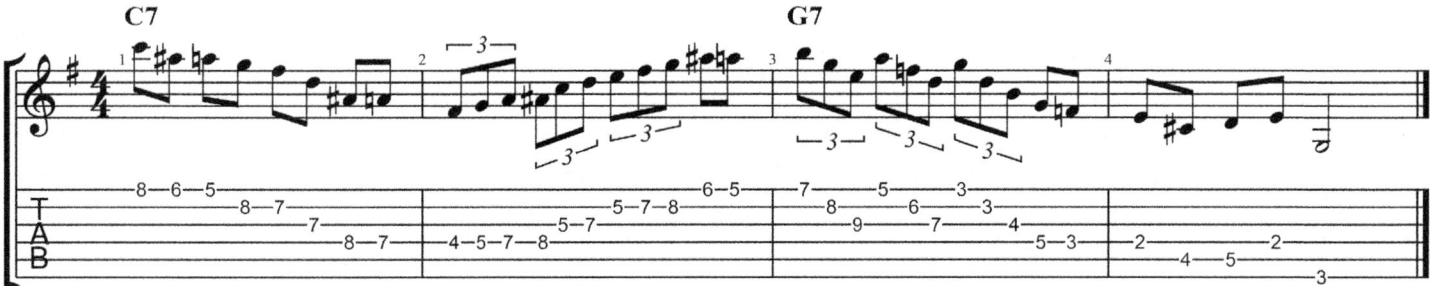

Let's look at an alternative idea over the same four bars. This idea uses shapes located in the same zone of the neck, rather than connecting adjacent shapes. We start off using Shape 1 of G Melodic Minor, then move into Shape 3 of D Melodic Minor.

Both shapes occupy the frets 2-6 zone of the neck. This is a little more difficult to get your head around, so the diagrams below show how that looks. Spend some time improvising with these shapes and find a few different transition points between them.

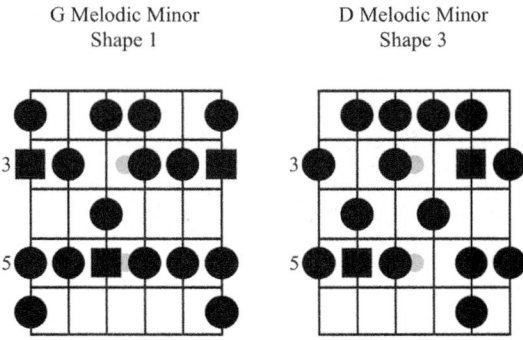

Example 4g

Now we come to the final four bars of the blues, where the V chord moves to the IV chord and back to the I chord. You'll immediately realize that this gives us musical options: we could improvise using a different melodic minor scale over every chord, or we could mix up blues vocabulary with just one melodic minor scale.

Here's a Wes Montgomery type idea to begin with. Wes would often spell out the V to IV movement with a motif-like phrase, like in *West Coast Blues*. This idea uses A Melodic Minor over the D7 chord, repeats the phrase down a whole step in G Melodic Minor over the C7, then ends with a bluesy phrase.

Example 4h

This line uses G Minor Pentatonic vocabulary over the D7 bar, then expands into G Melodic Minor for the C7 chord, and finally transitions into D Melodic Minor for the G7.

Example 4i

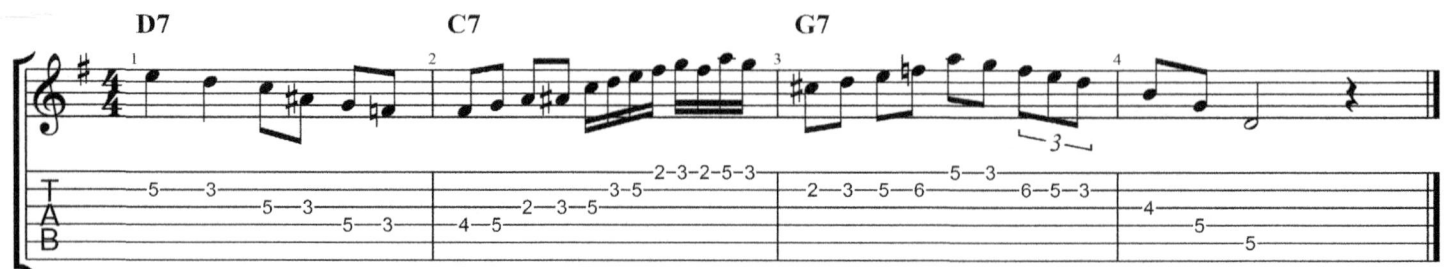

To end this chapter, here's a full chorus of a blues in G, utilizing all the ideas we've discussed. The notation indicates what scale or idea is being used at a given point, i.e., D Melodic Minor Shape 4 is used throughout bars 1-2, etc.

Example 4j

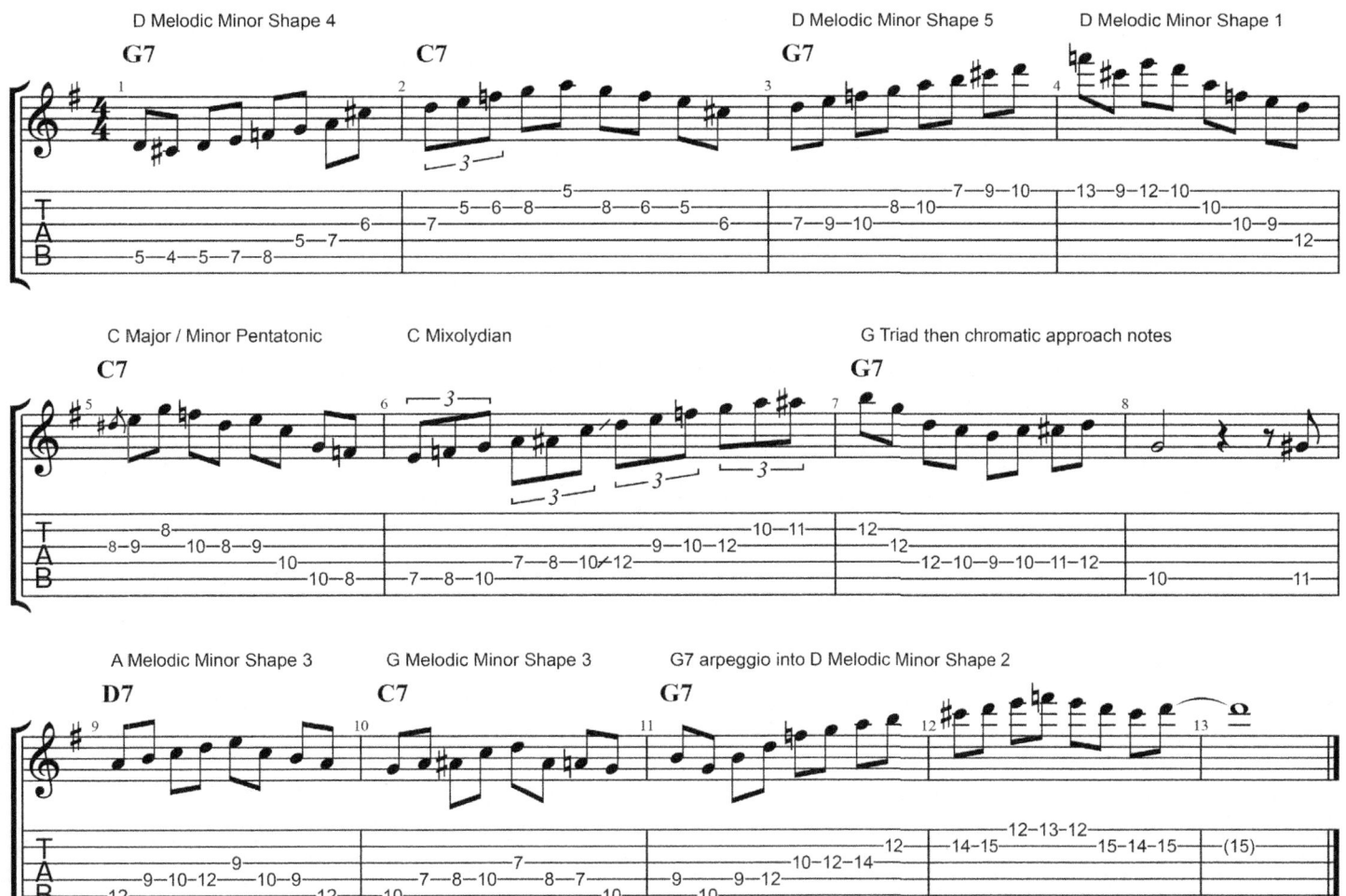

I'll be honest, when I first started practicing this idea with my guitar mentor, Adrian Ingram, I spent the next two years just practicing it over the blues, until playing the melodic minor up a 5th became so automatic, I didn't have to think about it anymore. The truth is, there is a lot of harmonic territory to explore here – and that's beside the task of learning how to move between the melodic minor scale in different key centers. But it's one of the most rewarding things I've ever worked on and, if you persevere with it, I think you'll find the idea to be a game-changer.

Chapter Five – Perfect 5th Above a Minor 7 Chord

In the jazz repertoire there are a number of must-know modal tunes that have multiple bars of minor chords to solo over. As well as the obvious *So What* and *Impressions*, we have Wayne Shorter's *Footprints*, Freddie Hubbard's *Little Sunflower*, and Miles Davis' *Milestones,* to name a few.

An obvious choice would be to play D Melodic/Harmonic Minor over the static Dm7 chord of *So What,* but we're going to try a different approach. Playing the harmonic minor scale a perfect 5th above that Dm7 chord (A Harmonic Minor over Dm7), yields some beautiful, moody, melodic results.

Why it works

A Harmonic Minor contains every chord tone of Dm7, then adds the 9th (E) and 13th (B) extended tones, plus a tense b5 (G#) tone.

We're going to take a similar approach to the previous chapter by first exploring this sound over a static Dm7 chord, then applying the idea to a minor blues.

It's time to revisit our A Harmonic Minor shapes! This ascending line uses Shape 1 exclusively. Have a careful listen to the intervals that the scale tones create over the underlying Dm11 chord.

Example 5a

This line is based on Shape 2 of the scale and ends by resolving to a Dm11 chord tone (A, the 5th).

Example 5b

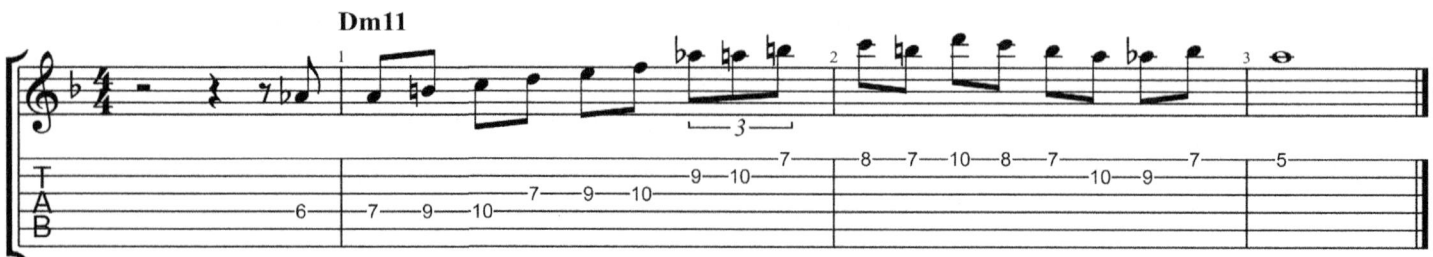

Both the previous ideas were quite linear in construction, so let's mix things up a bit more. This lick uses Shape 3 and develops a descending motif idea, ending the line on a B note, which implies a Dm6 sound.

Example 5c

Now let's continue exploring this sound by playing it over the changes of the popular minor blues tune *Mr. PC* by John Coltrane in D Minor. We'll take four bars at a time and play a couple of ideas over each section.

We begin on the chord Dm7, so we'll continue to create lines with A Harmonic Minor. However, we now need to extend our ideas to span four bars.

Example 5d uses Shape 1 of the scale and ends on an E note (the 9th of D minor).

Example 5d

Here's an alternative idea over the first four bars. This is the kind of sequential idea Kurt Rosenwinkel might play and moves through the harmonic minor scale shapes in order, beginning in Shape 1, using notes on the top two strings to create a motif.

Example 5e

Now we move onto the next four-bar section of the *Mr. PC* changes. Here, the chords are two bars of G minor followed by two bars of D minor.

This means our scale choices are D Harmonic Minor (a 5th above the Gm11 chord) and back to A Harmonic Minor for the Dm11. We can of course mix these up with simple D Minor Pentatonic ideas for variety.

We've not attempted D Harmonic Minor yet, so here are the shapes, ordered from low to high on the neck.

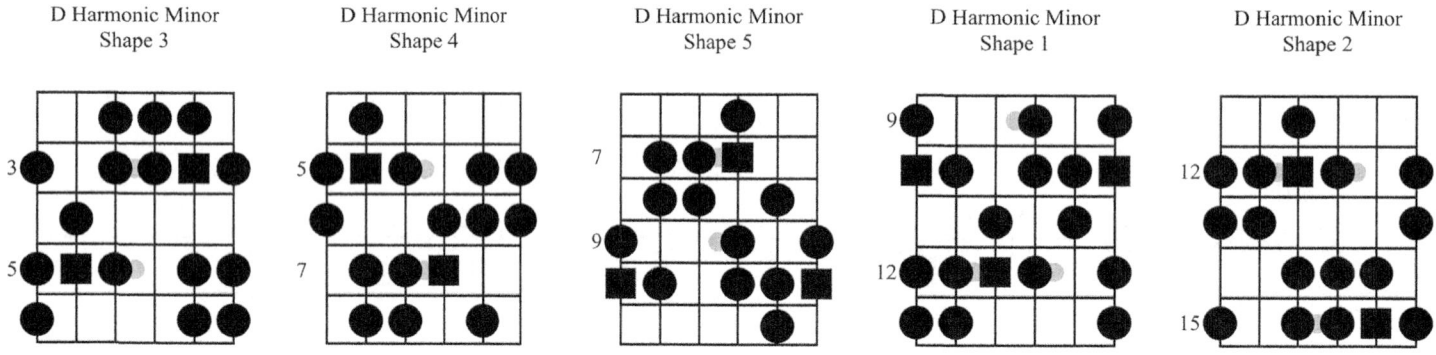

This example moves from D Harmonic Minor Shape 1 into A Harmonic Minor. Note the tied notes that float over the bar line to give this line a cool, laid-back feel.

When we explored the idea of using multiple substitute tonal centers earlier, we noted that it takes quite a bit of brain power and strong grasp of fretboard visualization to pull off. Knowing your scale shapes really well is the key to success here. Isolating ideas is also a big help. You could write out the D Harmonic and A Harmonic minor scales, side by side, on a single sheet of paper and use this as your crib sheet while you practice moving between them.

Example 5f

Over the Gm11 chord, this idea is constructed around Shape 4 of D Harmonic Minor. In bar three, it transitions into Shape 1 of A Harmonic Minor. In bar four, the phrasing of the previous bar is mimicked, but we've broken away from the harmonic minor to play a Dm9 arpeggio-based idea.

Example 5g

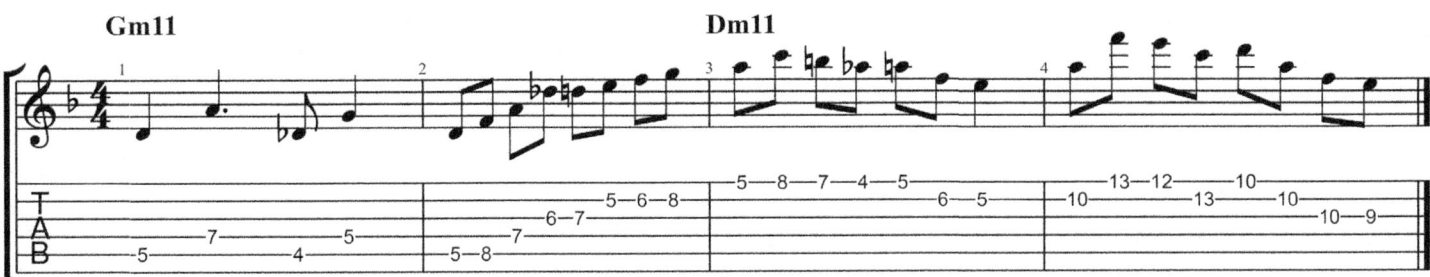

Now let's explore a couple of ideas over the final four-bar section of this minor blues. In the *Mr. PC* changes, the chords here are:

| Bb7 | A7 | Dm11 | % |

In the key of D Minor, the A7 chord doesn't belong (it should be Am7), but all three chords *do* belong to the harmonized key of D Harmonic Minor. Technically, the Bb chord in the harmonized scale is Bbmaj7, but here Bb7 is being used as a chromatic approach chord that leads to A7. However, we have the Bb major triad in the scale to create melodic ideas that fit over Bb7.

Following our "5th above" substitution, we could play E Harmonic Minor over the A7 chord. We could also play a substitution over the Bb7 chord, but it would feel like we are just trying to crowbar in another idea. A better option for these two bars is simply to play the D Harmonic Minor parent scale, so that's what we'll do.

Our strategy for these four bars then, is to play two bars of D Harmonic Minor followed by two bars of A Harmonic Minor.

This line uses D Harmonic Minor Shape 4 for bars 1-2. The F and E notes at the end of bar two are shared by A Harmonic Minor Shape 2, so we can use them to transition into that shape for bars 3-4.

Example 5h

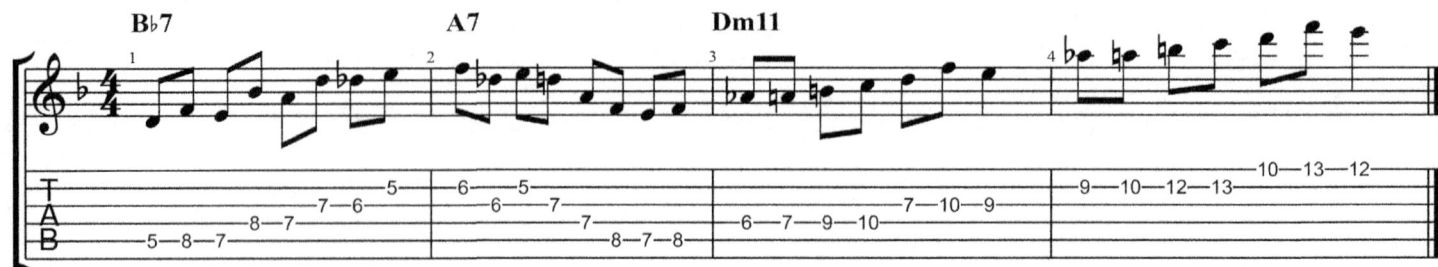

This line begins in Shape 5 of D Harmonic Minor. This time we find common notes with A Harmonic Minor Shape 1 on the second string, frets 5 and 6 to use as our transition point. In bars 3-4, we're playing an ascending A Harmonic Minor pattern on just the first string before resolving the line at the end.

Example 5i

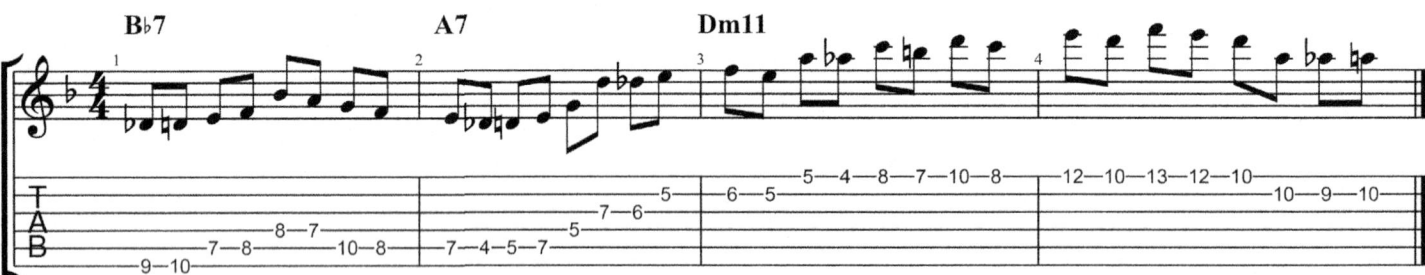

For the final example in this chapter, here's a way of navigating a full chorus of this minor blues, using the ideas we've explored. The scale choices and shapes are indicated in the TAB. I hope this inspires you to explore some new ideas over the minor blues form. It's all too easy to fall into minor pentatonic or Dorian clichés, and this harmonic minor substitution allows us to create something more harmonically interesting.

Example 5j

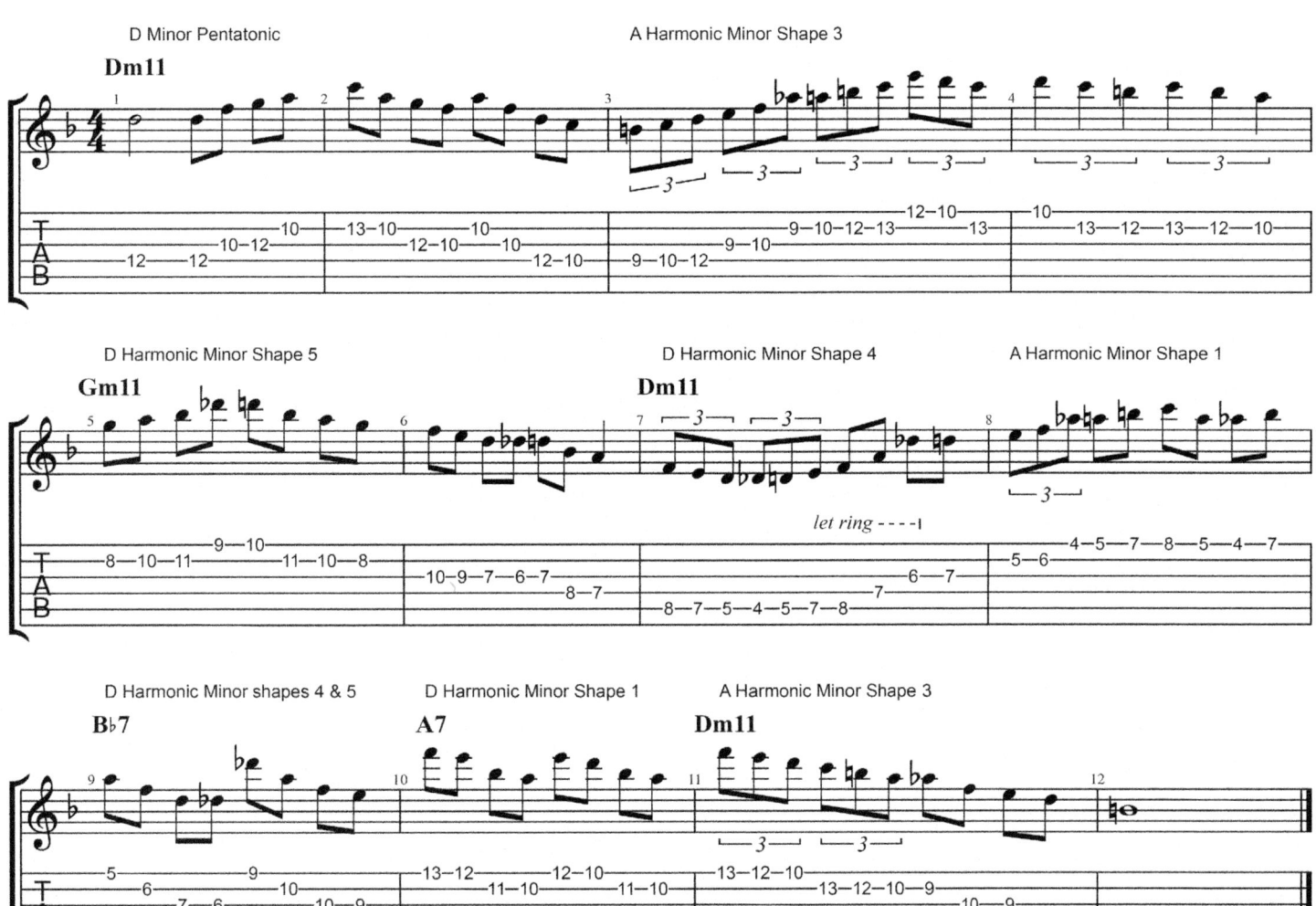

Chapter Six – Half Step Above the V Chord

Next, we come to one of the most used substitution ideas in jazz: to play a melodic minor scale a half step above the root of the V chord in a ii V I.

This idea is as effective as it is easy to remember and is a shortcut hack to creating the sound of the Altered scale.

Let's say we're playing over the sequence Em7 – A7 – Dmaj7. Over the A7 chord, we can play the Bb Melodic Minor scale, a half step up from the A root note.

Wonderfully, this idea works just as well in a minor ii V i setting, so if our chord progression is Em7b5 – A7#5 – Dm11, we can still play Bb Melodic Minor over the V chord.

In this chapter we'll explore this idea over both progressions. I chose them deliberately because it's good to keep changing key to really learn the scales. However, it shouldn't be too big a step to visualize the A Melodic Minor shapes you've learned moved up a half step to Bb.

By the end of this chapter, you'll have one scale that usefully serves two completely different harmonic contexts.

Why it works

Let's look at the notes of an A7 chord (A, C#, E, G) and see what effect the Bb Melodic Minor scale has when we superimpose it.

Bb Melodic Minor: Bb, C, Db, Eb, F, G, A

It has three notes in common with A7, and importantly they are the root, b3 and b7 – the defining chord tones: A, Db (C#) and G.

The rest of the notes offer us *every* possible way in which we can alter a dominant chord: the b9 (Bb), #9 (C), b5 (Eb) and #5 (F). Plus, it provides one extended note, the 13th (Gb).

Let's explore how this idea sounds over five major ii V I examples in the key of D Major.

Over the Em7 and Dmaj7 chords we'll use arpeggios and the D Major scale with a few passing notes thrown in to create the melodies and save the Bb Melodic Minor scale for the A7 chord.

Here's the first idea, which uses Shape 1 of Bb Melodic Minor (root note on the sixth string, 6th fret). Pause and digest the sound of this substitution. I'm sure it's one you've heard on modern jazz recordings, and the more you experiment with it, the more you'll begin to hear it in other musicians' playing.

Example 6a

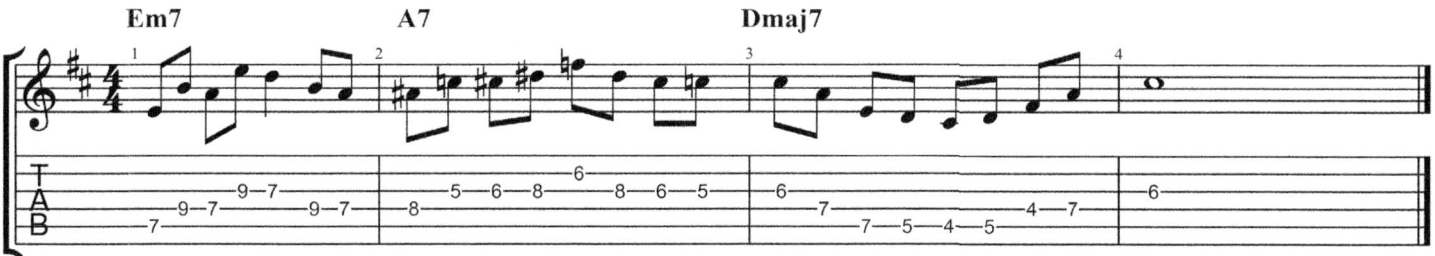

After ascending an Em7 arpeggio we use Shape 2 of Bb Melodic Minor (root note on the fourth string, 8th fret) over A7.

Example 6b

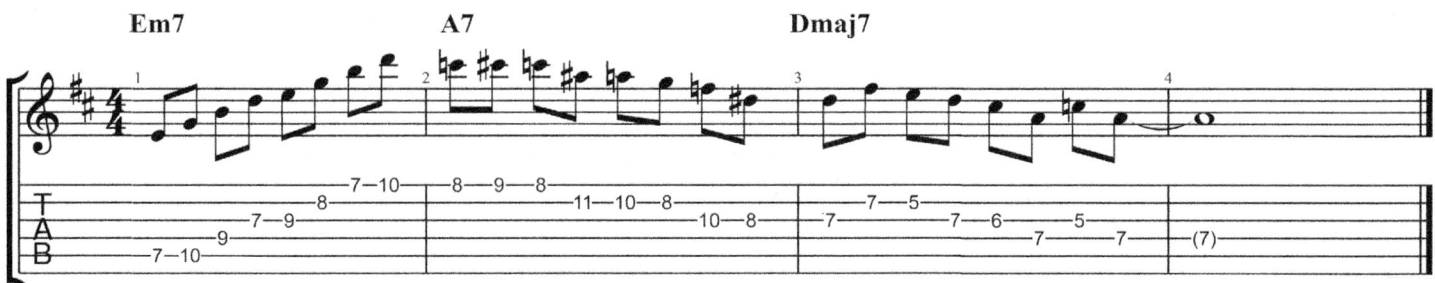

Where possible, half step connections will make our scale transitions sound very smooth. In bar two, we're using the top notes of Bb Melodic Minor Shape 1. At the end of bar one, the A note on the top string is shared by the D Major scale and Bb Melodic Minor, then the half step movement to the Bb note on the 6th fret tells our ears that something different is happening. At the end of bar two, the half step movement from the 6th to 7th fret tells our ears we're going back inside the harmony as we hit the F# note on beat 1 of bar three (the 3rd of Dmaj7).

Example 6c

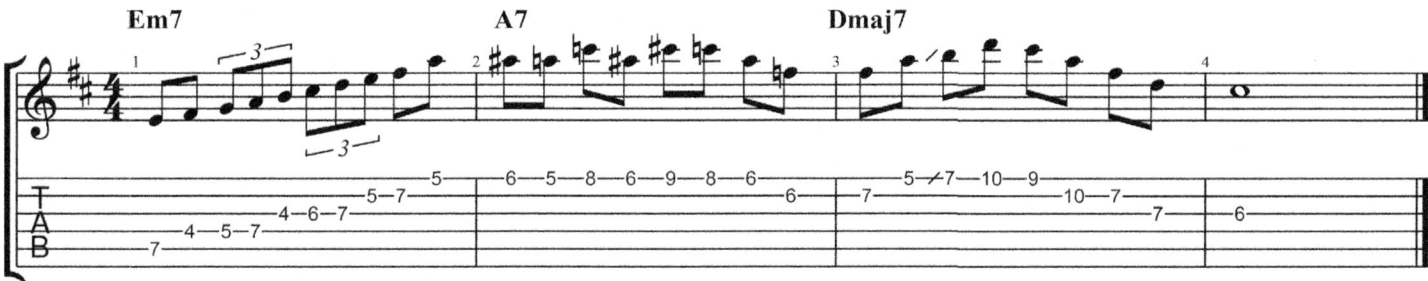

This example uses Shape 2 of Bb Melodic Minor organized into an 1/8th note triplet pattern, and we use a half step movement (top string, 11th to 12th fret) to move into a descending Dmaj7 arpeggio lick.

Example 6d

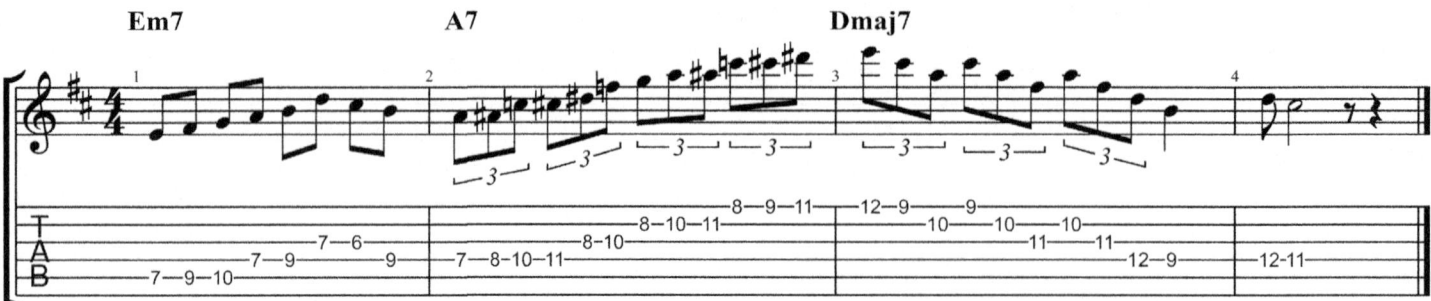

This more laid-back idea is based around Shape 5 of Bb Melodic Minor (root note on the sixth string, 6th fret, with the notes arranged below the root). Again, we're using half step movements to get in and out of the substituted scale.

Example 6e

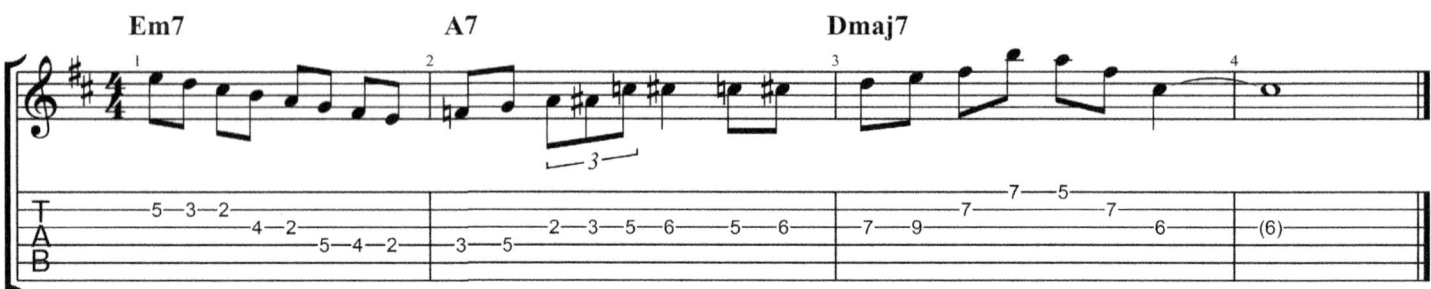

Now we turn to playing over a ii V i sequence in the key of D Minor. Although we're using the same scale over the same chord, the harmonic context is now completely different, and we have to connect our ideas to two different chords either side of the dominant 7. This instantly gives our lines a different flavor and makes the substitution idea sound fresh again.

Here, the first four notes ascend an Em7b5 arpeggio, then we create a melody with D Natural Minor scale notes. We get into Shape 1 of Bb Melodic Minor via a half step movement and get out of it with another on the top string to play a Dm7 arpeggio inversion.

Example 6f

Here's a more ambitious line that uses a 1/16th note run based around Shape 2 of Bb Melodic Minor (root note on the fourth string, 8th fret).

Example 6g

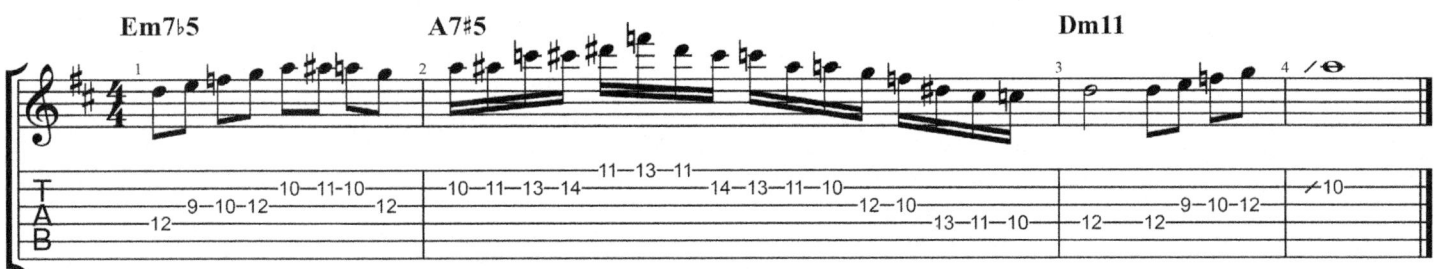

Here's another line with a 1/16th note run in Bb Melodic Minor over the A7#5 chord. This time we're connecting Shape 1 and Shape 2 of the melodic minor.

Example 6h

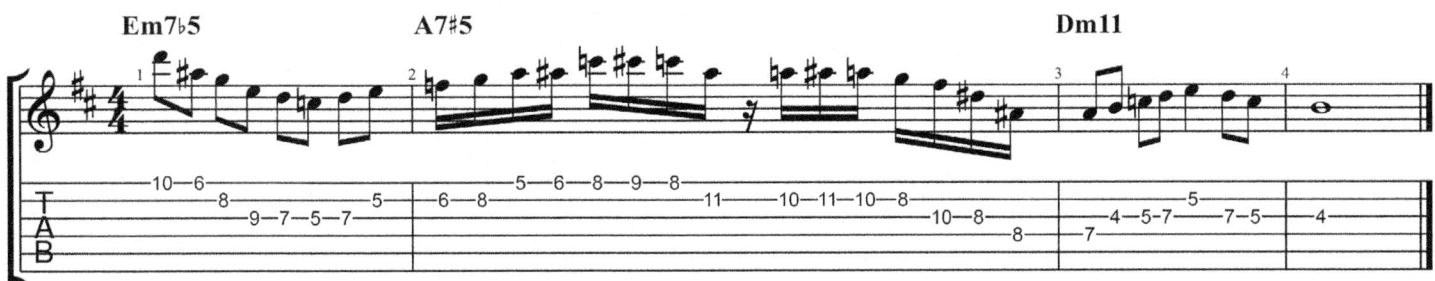

In this example we begin by sequencing the notes of an Em7b5 arpeggio, then move a half step up into Shape 5 of Bb Melodic Minor. For interest, in bar three we're borrowing the moody sounding B note of the D Dorian scale to add some color to the line over the D minor chord, which creates a Dm13 sound.

Example 6i

In this final idea, the line begins by using the D Natural Minor scale over Em7b5 but the last note of bar one anticipates the arrival of the Bb Melodic Minor scale in bar two. Here we're using Shape 3 (root note on the fifth string, 13th fret, with the notes arranged below the root). We end with a descending Dm9 arpeggio.

Example 6j

This substitution is such a prolific idea in modern jazz that it's worth dedicating a significant amount of practice time to ensure it becomes embedded in your melodic vocabulary.

Chapter Seven – A Minor 3rd Above the ii Chord

I had an epiphany when I discovered the modern jazz concept of moving melodic ideas around in minor 3rds and began to recognize just how much it is used in jazz. In its simplest form, it just involves playing a lick, then repeating it four frets higher, but one of the ideas that arises from this concept is to play a substitute scale a minor 3rd above a specific chord in a progression.

In this chapter, we're going to do that over the ii and V chords in the ii V I sequence. This is quite a useful, expansive idea because…

- We can play a minor scale a minor 3rd above the ii chord in a ii V I
- We can play the same scale over the V chord
- It works in both major and minor ii V I settings

As in the previous chapter, we're going to apply this concept over both major and minor ii V Is. However, this particular idea works best if we use the *melodic* minor scale for the major ii V I and the *harmonic* minor scale for the minor ii V i.

We'll change key again to give you some more practice at transposing the scales around the fretboard and play in the keys of C Major and C Minor.

Over the sequence Dm7 – G7 – Cmaj7 we'll use the F Melodic Minor scale (F is a minor 3rd interval above D).

Over the sequence Dm7b5 – G7#5 – Cm11 we'll use the F Harmonic Minor scale.

Why it works

At this point we could go into forensic detail and compare the notes of both scales to the notes of both sets of ii and V chords. But that's a lot of information and knowing it won't help you to play more melodically. Instead, it's better that we use our ears and pay attention to the tension notes we like the sound of.

However, I will summarize the theory by saying that if we play F Melodic Minor over the chords Dm7 and G7, the scale contains three chord tones of each chord, plus a selection of extended/altered tensions. The same is true when we play F Harmonic Minor over Dm7b5 and G7#5 chords.

Let's get straight into the music and hear how this idea sounds, because I'm sure you're going to like it. The first five lines here use the F Melodic Minor scale over the major ii V I.

We used this scale back in Chapter Four, but here is a quick reminder of the shapes.

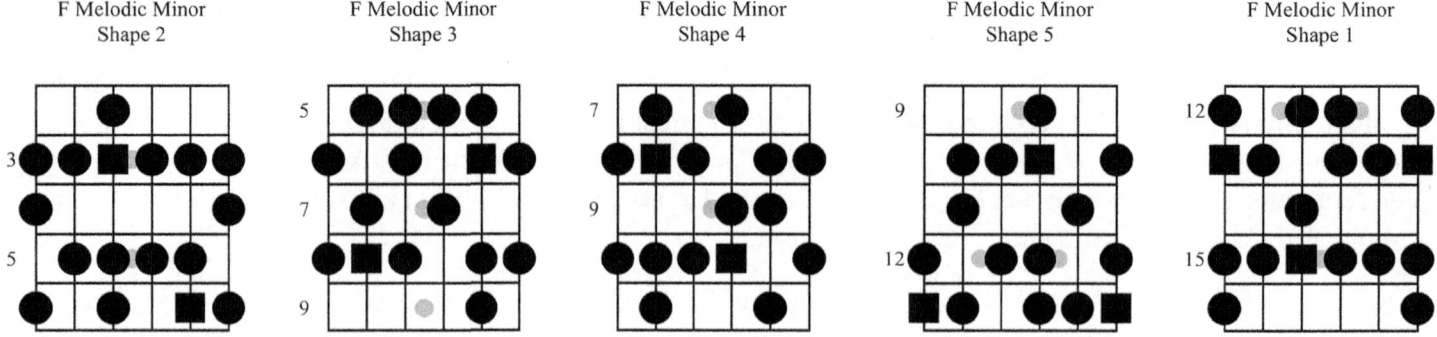

Remember that we're going to play the melodic minor scale over *both* ii and V chords, and each time we'll resolve to Cmaj7 arpeggios or the C Major scale to highlight the contrast between the two tonalities. Here is the first line.

Example 7a

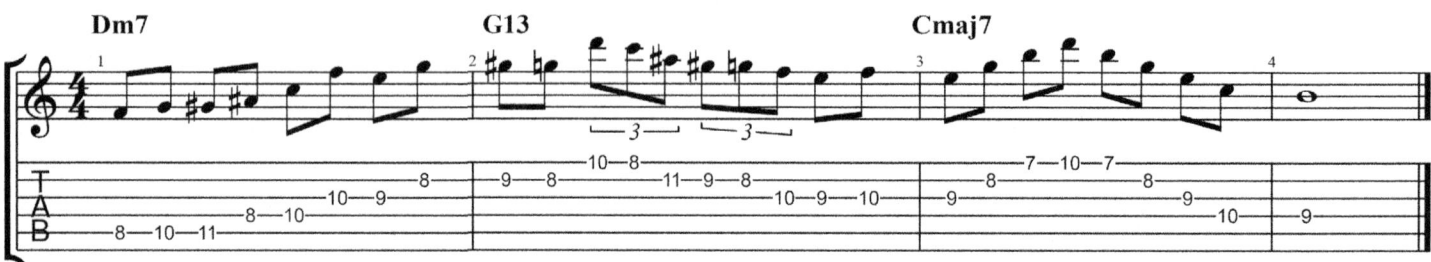

As you can hear, this substitution can instantly give our lines a more contemporary feel. It creates the sense that the melodic ideas are weaving around the chord tones in a more interesting way.

The line over Dm7 here sounds very angular, but not completely outside the harmony. We don't need a method of transition between bars 1-2, because it's all the melodic minor scale, but you'll notice we escape the scale with a half step movement into C Major at the beginning of bar three.

Example 7b

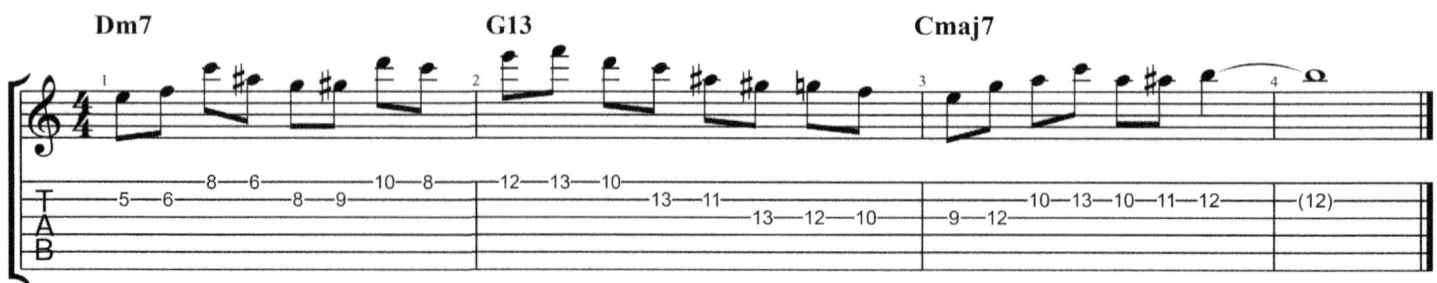

Here's an idea that begins with a fast 1/16th ascending run that moves through two shapes of F Melodic Minor in bar one. Can you see the transition point between the two? Bar two uses four adjacent melodic minor shapes as it descends, and we're just picking out triad clusters on the top three strings that exist within the shapes.

Example 7c

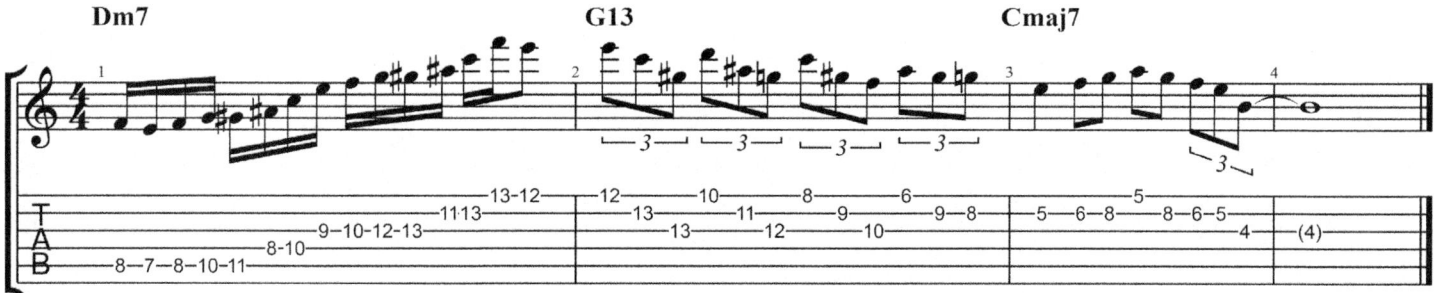

This line begins in Shape 1 of F Melodic Minor, but in open position, then moves into a fast run down Shape 2.

Example 7d

Depending on where we jump into a substitute scale, some of the phrases we play might sound quite dissonant. Especially if, for instance, we launch a line from the #5 (Bb) note. To counteract this, we can aim to launch the scale from a chord tone of the ii chord, like here, where we start from the D root note.

Example 7e

Now it's time to explore the sound of F Harmonic Minor, played over a ii V i in the key of C Minor. Here are the F Harmonic Minor shapes for reference, ordered low to high.

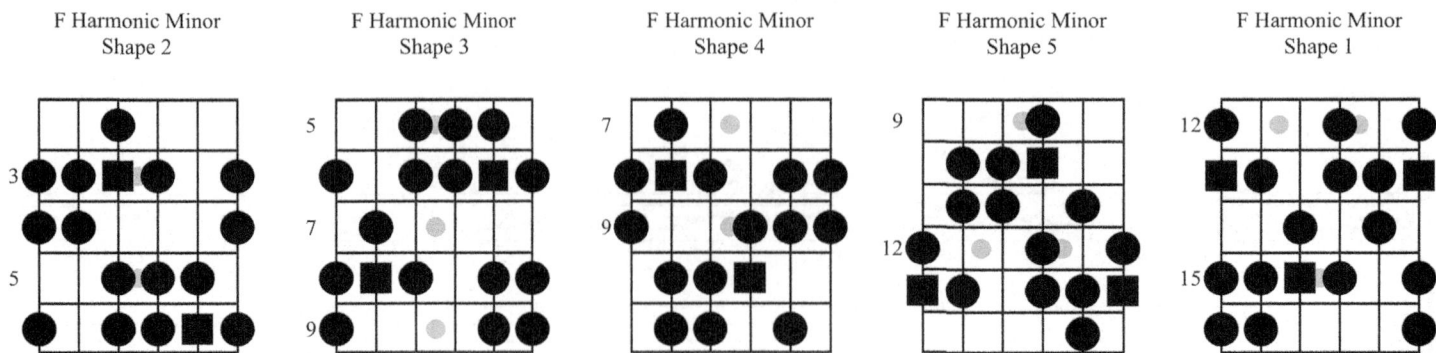

As in the previous set of examples, here we are playing the substitute scale over both the ii *and* V chords, then moving into C Natural Minor or C Dorian for the i chord.

This first line takes advantage of the parallel notes that sit on adjacent strings in Shape 3 and Shape 4.

Example 7f

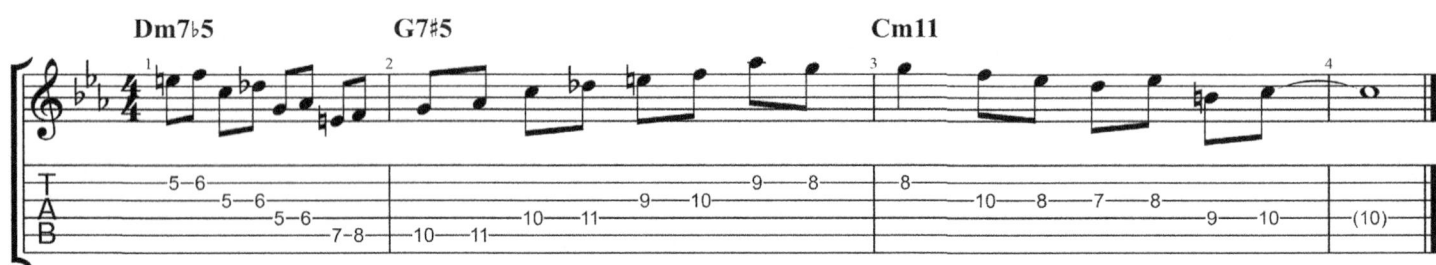

Here, we begin by picking out two triads that sit within the F Melodic Minor scale – first F minor then Ab augmented. In bar two we revert to a scalar approach. The more you explore this scale, the more you'll begin to see the shapes that are hidden inside it.

Example 7g

This line begins on the Ab note of F Harmonic Minor (the b3 of Dm7b5). In the transition from bar two to three, although the notes are located on different strings, this is still a half step movement.

Example 7h

Here's an F Harmonic Minor repeating pattern that descends using shapes 2 and 3. Once you know the pattern of the shapes inside out, you'll be able to construct your own similar sequenced ideas.

Example 7i

String skipping ideas test our scale shape knowledge, so this line uses that idea to close out this chapter.

Example 7j

Part 3 – More Modern Sounds

So far, we've explored several common substitution ideas that form the foundation of classic bebop and modern jazz. In this section we're going to explore more contemporary sounds – ideas you'll hear in the language of jazz guitarists such as Kurt Rosenwinkel, Gilad Hekselman, Jonathan Kreisberg, Mike Moreno and Lage Lund.

Chapter Eight – Harmonic Minor Over a Major 7 Chord

Whenever we play a substitution idea, it's tempting to want to resolve it as quickly as possible back to the safety of the "home" tonal center. But it seems to me that one thing that sets apart the new generation of modern jazz guitarists is that they're not afraid to continue playing interesting tensions over the home chord. This creates interest in their playing as they produce more challenging harmonies and more modern sounds.

In the next few chapters, we'll look at how to achieve this kind of sound, and begin with a harmonic minor scale substitution for the I chord in the major ii V I.

We'll change key again to explore this. Refer to your scale shape diagrams and use the root notes to transpose the shapes.

Let's say we want to improvise over the progression Fm7 – Bb7 – Ebmaj7.

For the Ebmaj7 chord, we're going to play the C Harmonic Minor scale.

For ease of memorization, let's call this the "relative minor substitution". In other words, we know that the relative minor key to Eb Major is C Minor, so over Ebmaj7 we play C Harmonic Minor.

That said, it's worth noting how a modern jazz guitarist such as Kurt Rosenwinkel thinks technically about this idea…

Why it works

One of the ideas that crops up in the playing of the new generation is turning to other keys to "borrow" chords, over which the parent scale is then played.

The whole idea of this particular substitution is to create a major 7#5 sound over the I chord. The chord Ebmaj7#5 occurs naturally in the harmonized C Harmonic Minor scale, where it is chord iii.

This then, is the chain of logic that leads to us playing C Harmonic Minor over the I chord in the sequence Fm9 – Bb13 – Ebmaj7.

That said, we can play C Harmonic Minor over the *whole* progression. That might sound a bit crazy to begin with, but I think you'll like the sound of it once you begin to experiment.

For practice, write out the five shapes of C Harmonic Minor and make yourself a reference chart for this chapter.

Now let's explore this sound.

This line begins in Shape 3 of C Harmonic Minor in the lower register. It moves into Shape 4 in bar two, keeping the notes sparse, then into Shape 5 in bar three.

Example 8a

This line uses the idea that wherever there are two notes on adjacent frets on the same string, we play the higher note first then drop a half step to play the next. The note B is the #5 in the chord Ebmaj7#5 and that tonality is emphasized at the end of this lick.

Example 8b

Here is a modern triadic approach to playing over this sequence with the C Harmonic Minor scale. Thought of simply, we're just moving through successive scale shapes and picking out fragments of each shape using three notes that fall on adjacent strings.

Viewed harmonically, these are all triad forms that spell out chords belonging to the harmonized key of C Harmonic Minor. E.g., in bar one we have Cmin(Maj)7, then Abmaj7. In bar two we have Ebmaj7#5 then Fm7, etc.

Example 8c

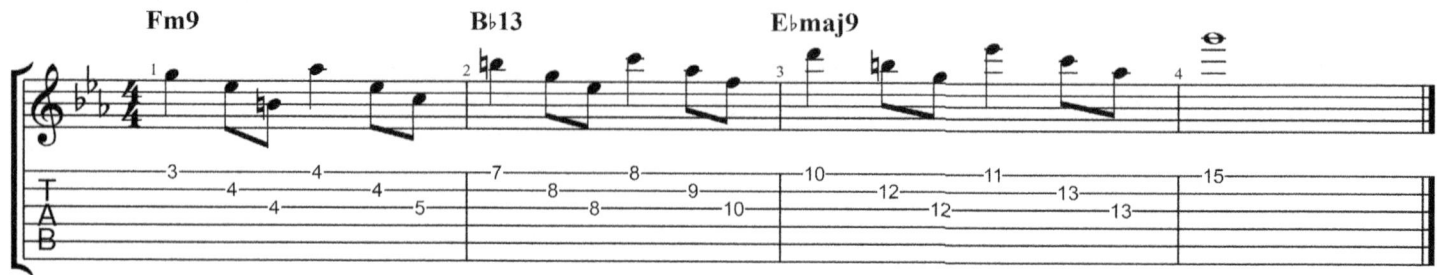

This line begins by ascending Shape 1, then shifts down to Shape 5 in bar two. We move down again to Shape 4 in bar three. The line ends on a D note (the major 7 of the chord). The fact that it's played in the lower register, and is a half step below the root, makes it sound more exotic than it is.

Example 8d

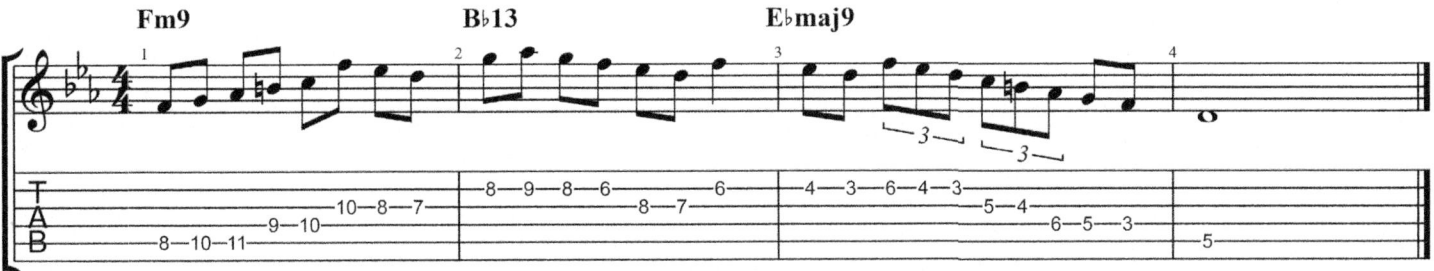

Example 8e is a pattern-driven idea using the notes of C Harmonic Minor, and visually you can see how the idea is laid out on the fretboard.

In bar one, the first four notes make an F diminished sound, but the last note immediately resolves to a chord tone of Fm9. In bar two, although a similar shape is played to begin with, the first four notes are all chord tones of Bb7 and the last note moves to the 11th of the chord.

In bar three, the way these three-note clusters are organized creates an Eb augmented sound over the Eb bass note. It's the #5 note (B) that achieves this effect and it appears four times in this bar.

Example 8e

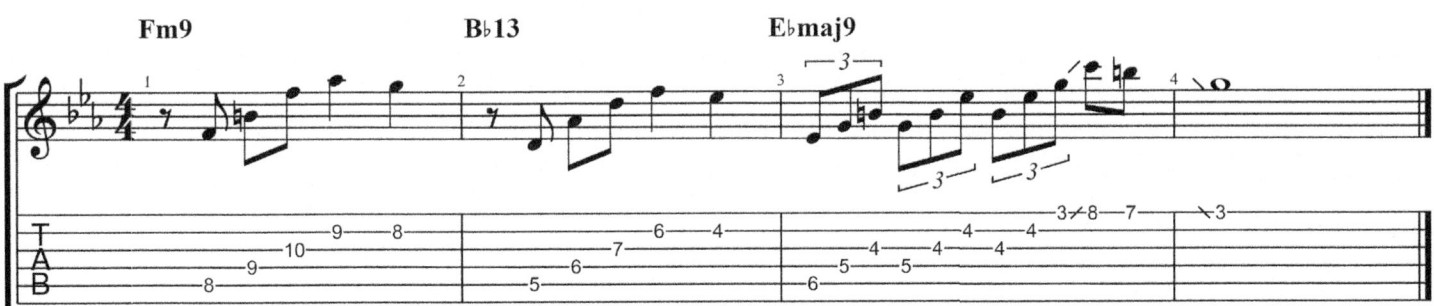

It's always good to look for patterns in scale shapes as these can lead to some interesting musical ideas. If we then apply rhythm, it can help us to avoid simply running up and down the shapes. This is another line that lands unashamedly on the #5 at the end.

Example 8f

This idea begins in Shape 2, moves down into Shape 1, skips the adjacent Shape 5, and jumps into Shape 4 for the Ebmaj9 chord. As a result, it uses a wide range of the fretboard.

Example 8g

It's time for a more challenging lick. Visually, you can see that in bar one, the lick is based on the idea of taking a four-note motif and ascending the scale on the second and third strings. The line breaks into a scale run idea in bar two, descending then ascending. Watch out for the 1/16th note rest halfway through – it introduces a "breath" into the line and means that the second half is of unequal length. We slow things right down in bar three and the line ends on the major 7 of Ebmaj9.

Example 8h

In this idea, we take a similar approach to Example 8c, but this time we're using four-note clusters in bars 2-3. In bar two, the two sets of note clusters look like Eb augmented inversions, but over the Bb bass note they make a Bb altered dominant sound. In bar three, the first four notes spell Ebmaj7#5, then we revert to the Eb augmented shape, resolving once again to the major 7 of Ebmaj9.

Example 8i

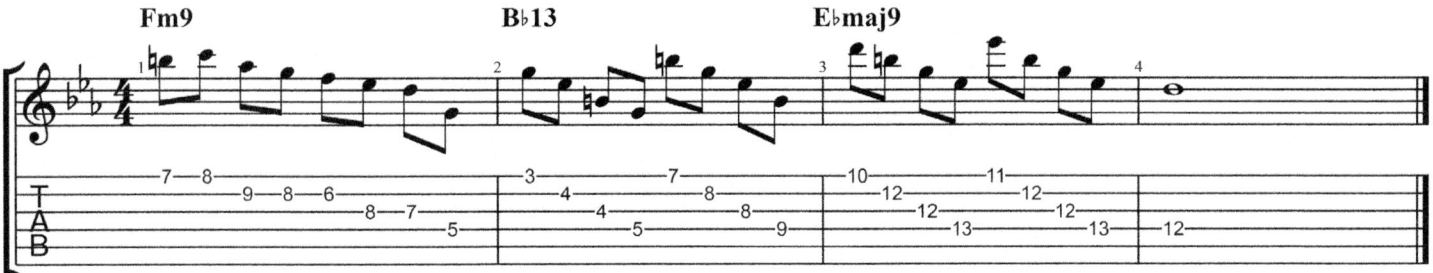

Finally, an idea that mixes rhythms to add a more dynamic sound to a constantly flowing line. The lick shifts between shapes 5 and 1 of C Harmonic Minor.

Example 8j

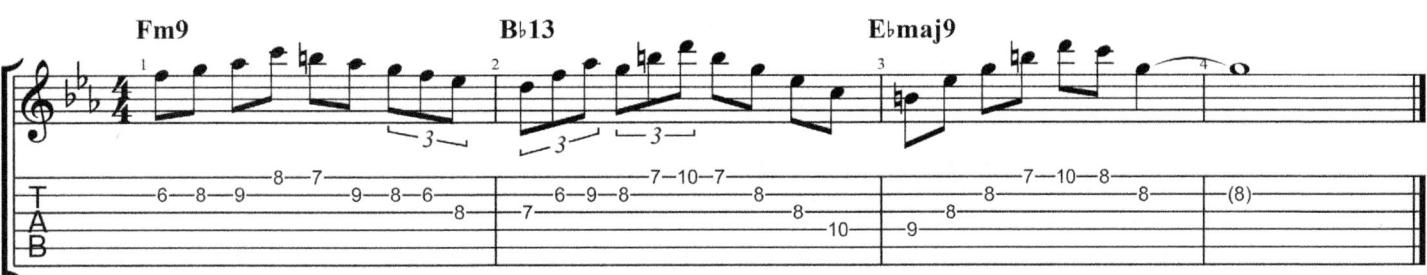

Chapter Nine – Parallel Key Melodic Minor

Searching for melodic material in parallel keys is an idea that both Kurt Rosenwinkel and Jonathan Kreisberg speak about. It is a similar idea to the one used in the previous chapter, but now the common link between scales is just the root note.

A parallel key means a key based on the same tonic note, regardless of the quality of the scale. For example, C Major and C Natural Minor.

In this chapter, we're going to play over a ii V I in the key of C Major (Dm7 – G7 – Cmaj7), but draw our musical vocabulary from the key of C Melodic Minor (C, D, Eb, F, G, A, B).

The harmonized C Melodic Minor scale has two chords in common with C Major, and they happen to be Dm7 and G7.

Playing C Melodic Minor over Cmaj7 creates some undesirable tensions, but we can use this idea to form a soloing strategy over the major ii V I that involves moving seamlessly between C Melodic Minor and C Major.

Not only is this a great sounding transition, it's one that is easy to negotiate on guitar. And if we want to keep things sounding really contemporary, we can also go from C Melodic Minor to C Lydian. We'll try both in this chapter.

Why it works

Dm7 and G7 chords are diatonic to C Melodic Minor, so the scale contains all the notes of both chords. In addition, it provides some nice extensions/alterations:

For Dm7 it's the b9 (Eb), 11th (G) and 13th (B)

For G7 it's the 9th (A), 11th (C) and #5 (Eb)

First, let's explore the approach of transitioning from C Melodic Minor to C Major through five lines.

We've not used C Melodic Minor shapes so far in this book, so take some time to create a crib sheet for yourself.

You'll hear right away that using C Melodic Minor over the ii V change here makes the ears prick up – especially the b9 tension over the Dm7 chord. Dominant 7 chords can withstand more alterations, so the line in bar two just sounds like an altered dominant lick. Stick with the tensions on the ii chord though, they grow on you!

Example 9a

It can help to get your head around a substitution idea if you emphasize underlying chord tones to begin with, as is the case here in bar one, where the lick begins and ends on the D root.

Example 9b

In this line, the tensest sounding note over Dm7 is saved for beat 4& of bar one, so that we treat it like a passing note. In bar three, we stray away from the C Major scale slightly to play an old favorite bebop lick that includes a passing note.

Example 9c

The idea in bars 1-2 of Example 9d is to build ascending runs launching from chord tones. In bar one, it's the b3 (F) of Dm7 and in bar two it's the 5th (D) of G7. There is another bebop-style lick in bars 3-4.

Example 9d

Here's a faster idea to get your teeth into. The lick in bar one is based entirely around C Melodic Minor Shape 2 and remains in position throughout. We continue with this shape for bar two. Bar three is a sequenced C Major scale idea.

Example 9e

In the next set of five licks, we're going to move from C Melodic Minor (bars 1-2) to the C Lydian scale (C, D, E, F#, G, A, B) over Cmaj7.

C Lydian is a popular choice for soloing over major 7 chords to create a more open, less resolved sound. It has just one note different to C Major (its distinctive raised 4th degree, an F# instead of F), which gives it a spacey kind of sound. Check it out – I think the combination of these two scales really gives the ii V I a modern twist and helps us to escape the clichés inherent in focusing on the major key center to compose our ideas.

Example 9f

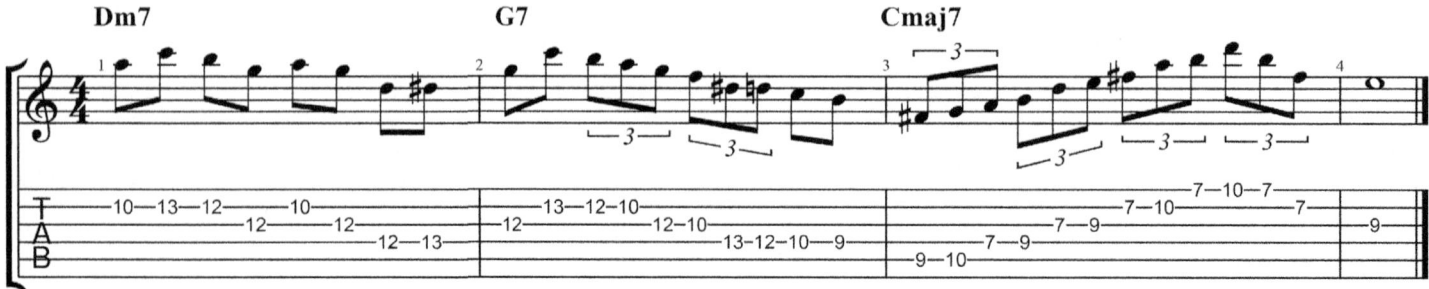

In the previous chapter we used the strategy of picking note clusters out of adjacent scale shapes to play triad/arpeggio ideas and we're doing it again here. It's those augmented shapes again, which create an altered dominant sound. In bar three, we deliberately land on the raised 4th (F#) note over Cmaj7 to highlight the Lydian sound and imply a Cmaj7#11 chord.

Example 9g

We're in Shape 2 again for this next line. First, an ascending/descending run that mixes 1/8th notes with 1/8th note triplets. Then, an intervallic idea in bar two, played in the same shape. For the Cmaj7 chord, an ascending run that targets the #11 chord sound at the end.

Example 9h

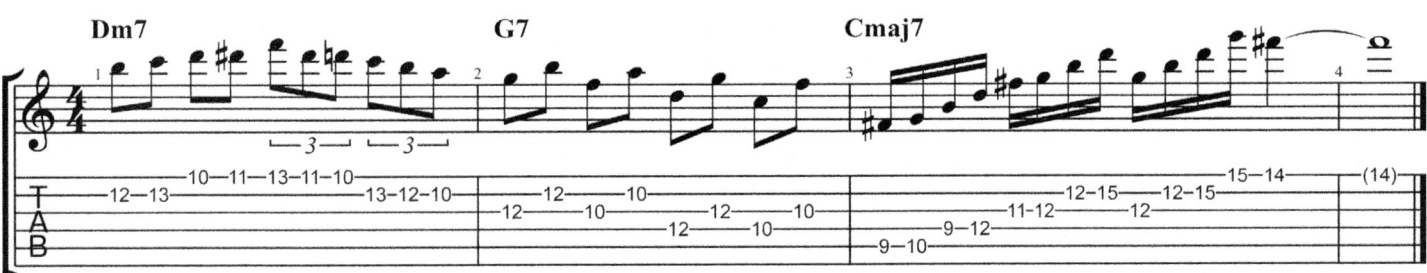

Here we're playing with triad clusters again to create a more angular, less linear sound over the chord changes. We can refer to our melodic minor shapes, but I also like to map the scale across the entire fretboard and examine it visually. Doing so often makes repeating shapes stand out, and these can instantly form the basis of melodic ideas.

Example 9i

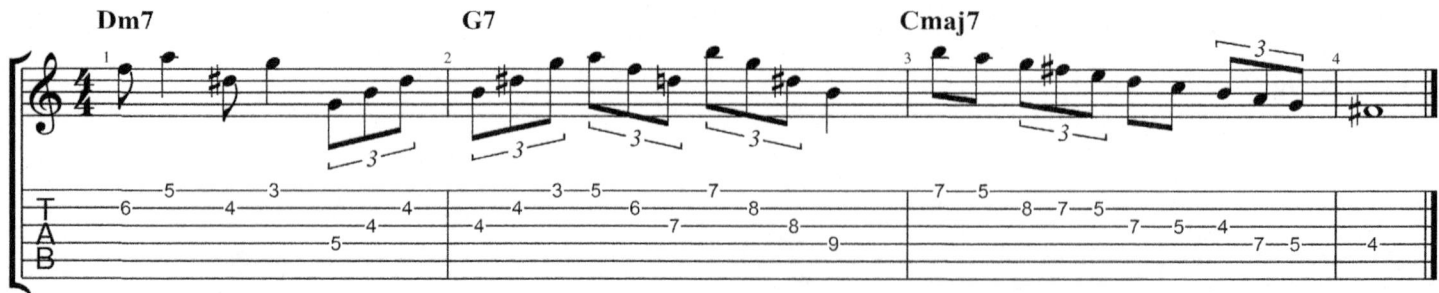

And, finally, an idea that weaves around the C Melodic Minor scale, before a faster C Lydian descending run to end on the 3rd of Cmaj7.

Example 9j

Chapter Ten – Minor 3rd Above a Dominant 7

Let's look at another minor 3rd movement idea. Previously we played a minor scale located a minor 3rd above the ii chord in the ii V I sequence. This time we're going to superimpose a minor scale located a minor 3rd above the V chord.

This means that over the sequence Dm9 – G7#5 – Cmaj9, we'll play the Bb Melodic Minor scale over the G dominant chord. (You'll recall that we got familiar with this scale in Chapter Six when we played it a half step above a V chord).

Why it works

The Bb Melodic Minor scale has the notes Bb, C, Db, Eb, F, G, A.

Compared to a G7 chord, the scale contains two chord tones (G and F, root and b7). Then it provides two extended notes, the 9th (A) and 11th (C), and three altered tones, the #9 (Bb), b5 (Db), and #5 (Eb).

Two of the tension notes this superimposition creates are rarely useful when played over minor chords, so we'll limit this substitution to being played over the V chord.

This actually sets up some nice movements for us on the fretboard. Depending on which zone of the neck we're playing in, we can slip between Bb Melodic Minor and C Major or C Lydian via either a half step or whole step movement.

If we're playing in the 5-8 fret zone, for example, C Major and Bb Melodic Minor shapes sit a half step apart. If we're playing C Major lines around 3rd position, we can shift down a whole step to 1st position to play Bb Melodic Minor. These pattern shifting opportunities add to the modern feel of the idea. Let's check it out…

Bar one begins with a Dm6 arpeggio, then we're playing Bb Melodic Minor Shape 1 in bar two. We end with a lick that highlights the Cmaj7#11 quality of C Lydian.

Example 10a

Bar two of this line arose from visualizing the Bb Melodic Minor scale mapped across the fretboard. These triplet clusters immediately bring out the altered tones of the scale superimposed over the G7 chord.

Example 10b

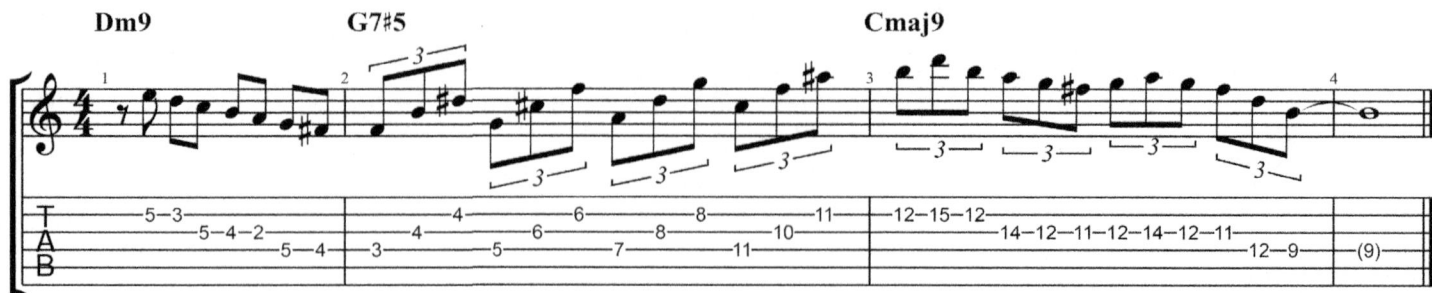

This is a motif-driven line that takes a simple idea played over the Dm9 chord, then shifts it down a whole step, adapting it to use the Bb Melodic Minor scale.

Example 10c

This positional lick takes advantage of the proximity of shapes in a single zone of the neck. Here we're moving from C Major to Bb Melodic Minor to C Lydian, all within a six-fret zone (a five-fret zone mostly, as only one note strays higher).

It obviously takes quite a bit of time and commitment to be able to visualize three different scales in a single zone, then work out how to move between them, and I'm not saying it's easy! If you persevere with this approach, however, it can yield some dramatic and musically pleasing moments.

Example 10d

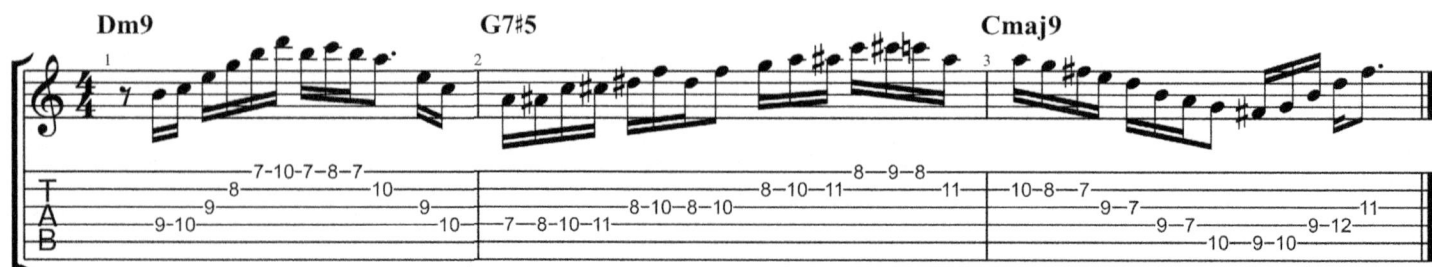

At the end of bar two in this line, we connect Bb Melodic Minor to C Lydian with a half step movement on the top string. Our first port of call should always be to look for the simplest transition point along one string, as this is likely to produce the most satisfying musical result.

Example 10e

Watch out for the "disrupted" rhythm in the descending run in bar one, where a lone 1/8th note breaks up the 1/16th note pattern. Again, in the transition between bars two and three, we make a half step movement into C Lydian. The A note over Cmaj9 produces a Cmaj13 sound.

Example 10f

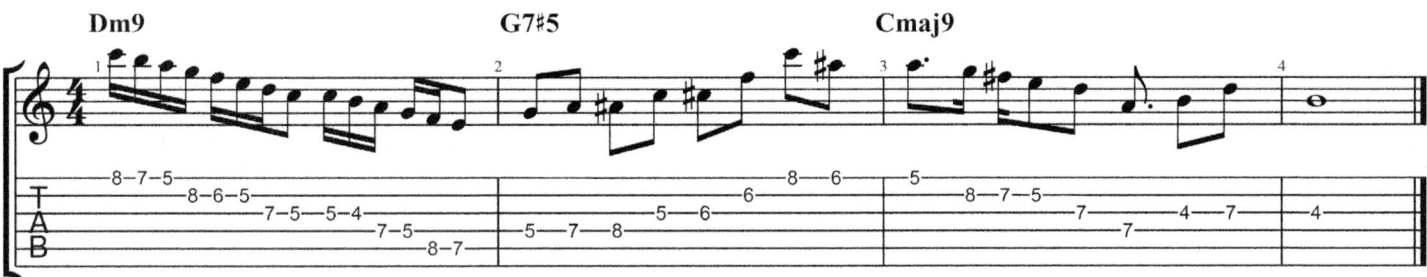

After arpeggiating the Dm9 chord in bar one, we play a back-stepping descending scale pattern in bar two to spell out the G altered dominant sound. In bar three, a C Lydian triadic idea completes the line.

Example 10g

This line creates a motif over the Dm9 chord in bar one, then adapts it for Bb Melodic Minor in bar two. Doing this gives any melodic idea a greater sense of continuity. It's amazing how our ears will accept altered tones if played with similar phrasing to some inside tones.

Example 10h

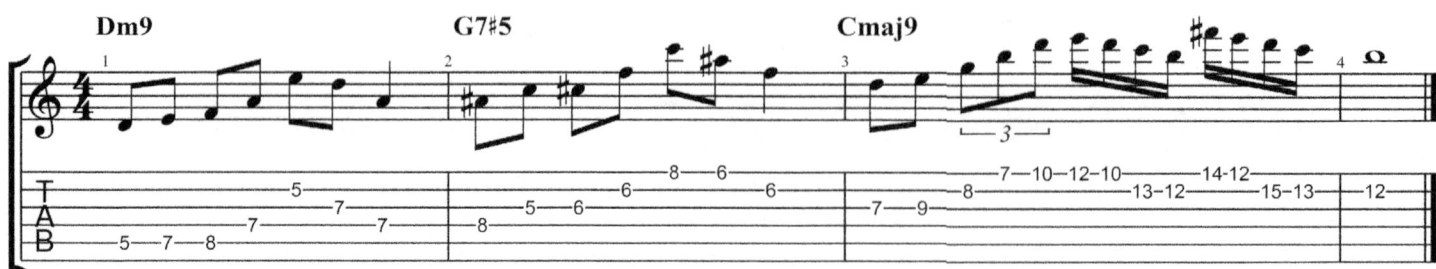

In this example, we play an ascending sequenced C Major lick over the Dm9, then a straight run down Bb Melodic Minor Shape 3 in bar two. To complete the lick, we have the C Lydian scale organized into 4th intervals.

Example 10i

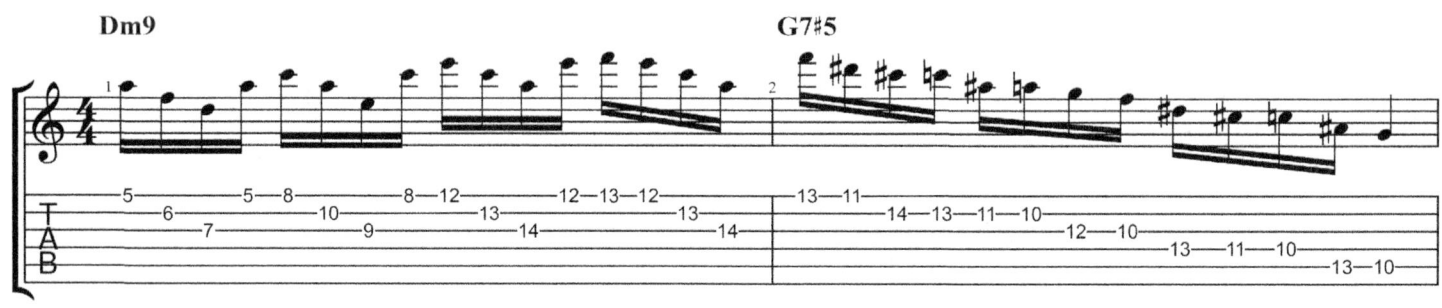

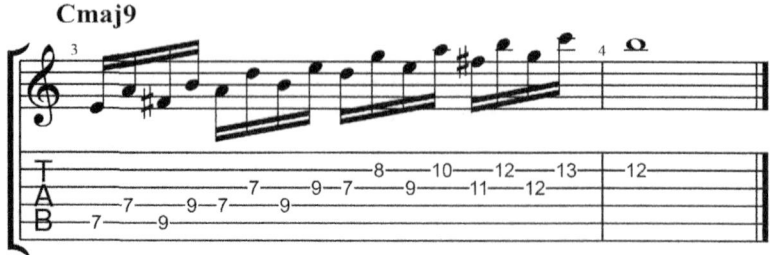

To finish this chapter, here's a line reminiscent of early Pat Metheny that ascends through the scale patterns mostly in 5ths and ends on the 9th of the C major chord.

Example 10j

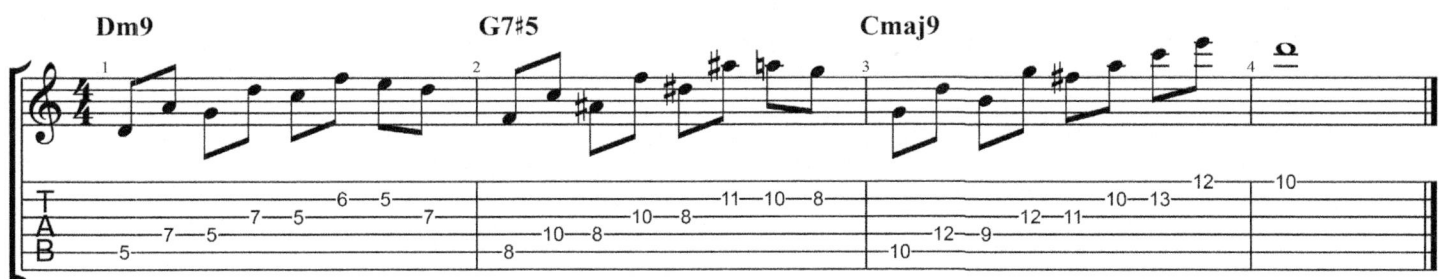

Part 4 – Performance Study

Chapter Eleven – How to Apply These Ideas to Your Playing

We've looked a lot of ways in which we can add harmonic and melodic minor vocabulary into our playing. I hope that some of these ideas immediately stood out to you, and you've been able to add them into your playing.

But, if you've arrived here feeling a little overwhelmed, perhaps thinking, "There are so many possibilities, where do I start?" or "How do I apply this to a standard?" that's exactly what we'll address in this chapter.

I find the best way to absorb new ideas into my playing is to take a jazz standard I'm familiar with, then go to town on it. In other words, I'll keep playing the changes and try *every* idea over them.

However – and this is the important part – I'll do so by introducing *one idea at a time.*

After thoroughly exploring one idea, only then will I add a second.

Then, I'll work with those two ideas for a while. Rather than paying lip service to them and quickly moving on, I'll really explore what those ideas have to offer. Because the longer we spend developing an idea, the more likely it is to naturally crop up when we're playing live music.

Having worked two ideas in tandem, I'll introduce a third, *but* I'll set aside one of the others for now.

You get the picture…

If you gradually introduce new ideas into your playing over time (I'm talking weeks and months here), and keep working on them, they are much more likely to stick and become a permanent feature of your jazz vocabulary.

In this chapter, we're going to use this method, albeit in compacted form. We'll take sections of a well-known jazz standard and examine the different ideas we can apply over the changes.

After we've been through the whole tune, you'll end up with a set of options you can pick and choose from – a palette of different color choices, if you like. When you set about improvising over the backing track, you can choose one option and work with it, then gradually introduce other ideas.

We're going to work with the chord changes to *My Funny Valentine* in the key of C Minor. I've chosen this piece because it has a rich harmony with some lovely chord changes, but it's also a ballad, which gives us more time to hear the effect of the substitution ideas being used.

(NB: If I'm working out how I want to solo over the changes of *any* tune, I always do a slow run-through – even if it's an up-tempo bebop piece. Slowing things down helps us to really hear and understand the harmony and gives us the chance to see how we can navigate our way through scale and arpeggio shapes on the fretboard).

Let's start simple and gradually build more complex ideas over this tune. For each example, I'll include a diagram to show the scale shape I'm using, and the scale choices will also be indicated in the TAB.

First, let's try a few different ideas over the first four bars.

Bars 1-4

The first four bars have the following chord changes:

| Cm | Dm7b5 G7b9 | Cm7 | F7 |

The chords Cm, Dm7b5 and G7 are all found in the key of C Harmonic Minor. The chords Cm7 and F7 are a ii V movement and imply that we're briefly in the key of Bb Major.

So, in this first example, we're using the C Harmonic Minor scale for bars 1-2 and the Bb Major scale for bars 3-4, which adds a Dorian flavor. The line is based around Shape 4 of C Harmonic Minor.

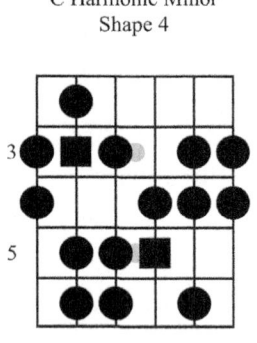

Example 11a

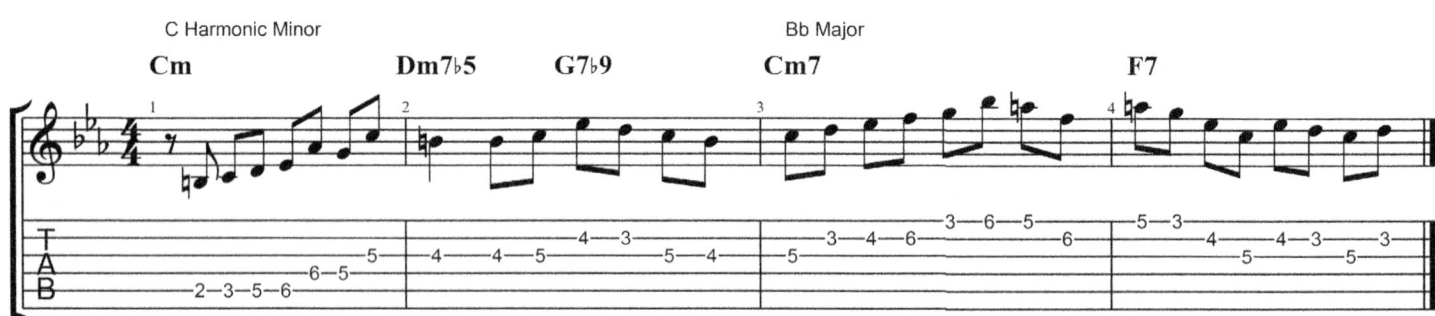

Here's a different idea over bars 1-4, taking the exact same approach, but this time using Shape 1 of C Harmonic Minor.

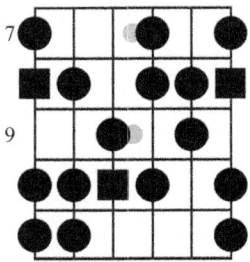

C Harmonic Minor
Shape 1

Example 11b

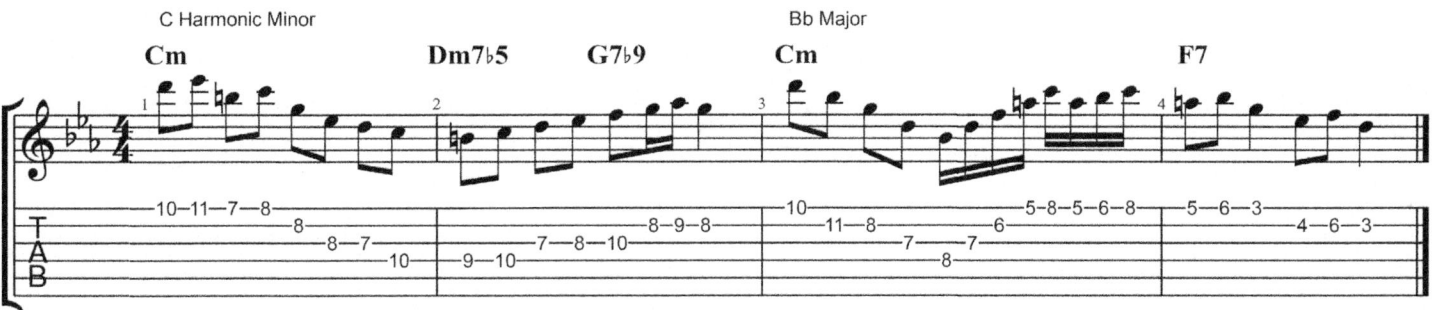

Remember that we're fast-forwarding the learning process here. I recommend you loop these four bars and explore playing *only* C Harmonic Minor and Bb Major over them for a good while before moving on.

However, because this chapter is a microcosm of our practice approach, we'll now play those four bars again and introduce a new idea. In bar one, we'll use C Harmonic Minor as before, and in bars 3-4 we'll use Bb Major again, but in bar two we'll play Ab Melodic Minor.

This is the melodic minor a half step above the dominant chord substitution (see Chapter Six). I.e., Ab Melodic Minor over G7b9.

We'll go back to Shape 4 of C Harmonic Minor and move into the adjacent Shape 1 of Ab Melodic Minor shown below.

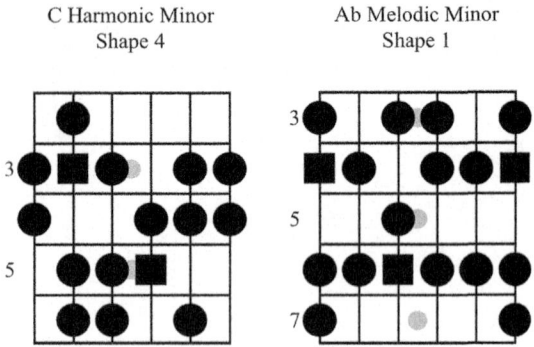

Example 11c

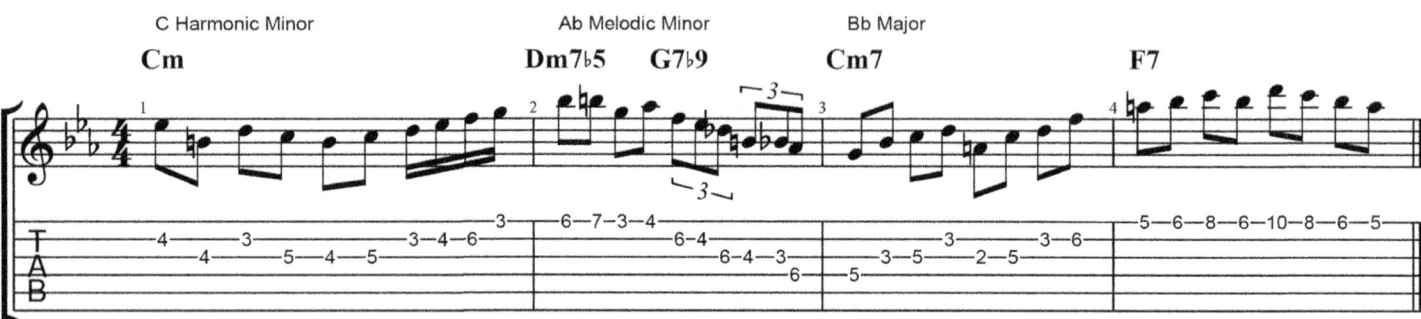

Let's play another line over this same section, using the exact same system and shapes. Dovetailing two different scale shapes located in the same zone of the fretboard is a great way to practice transitioning between them.

Example 11d

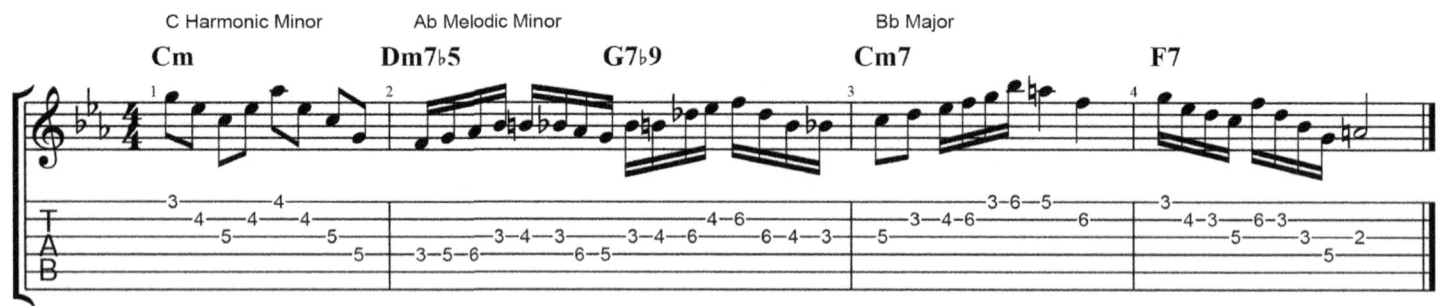

Bars 4-8

Now we move on to the next four-bar section of the tune. Here, the chord changes are:

| Abmaj7 | Fm7 | Dm7b5 | G7b9 |

Each of those chords belongs to the key of C Harmonic Minor, but we're going to introduce a new idea to play over bars 1-2.

Here we'll play F Harmonic Minor over the Abmaj7 – Fm7 change. (This is the "relative minor" substitution discussed in Chapter Eight). Then we're going to move into C Harmonic Minor over Dm7b5 – G7b9.

Again, we will use adjacent shapes for the two scales (shown below). It's worth practicing these shapes in sequence for a while, to get used to where the intervals lie and to note the similarities/differences between the scale shape layouts.

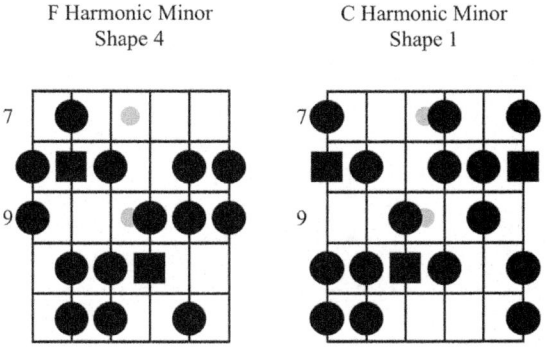

Example 11e

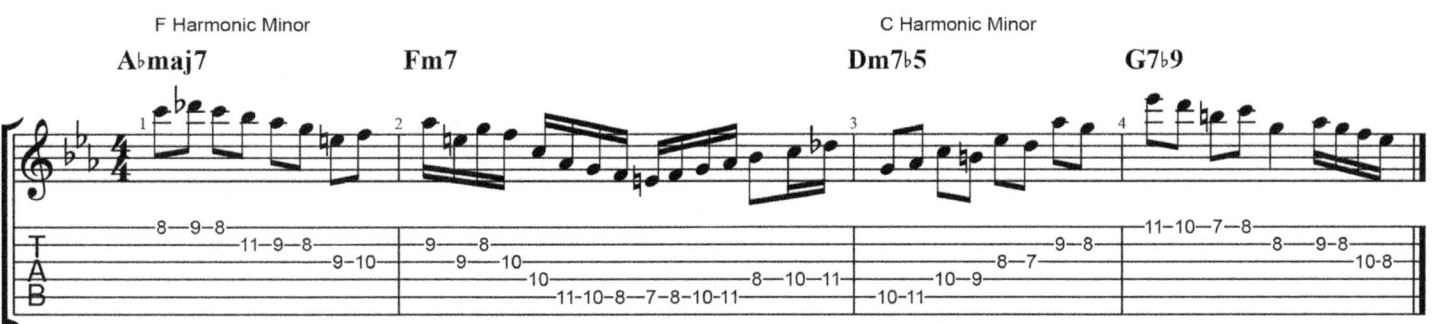

Let's try the same strategy over the same section. This time, however, we'll extend our use of the F Melodic Minor scale a bit further and use it to play over the Dm7b5 chord in the sequence too, because this chord naturally occurs in the key of F Melodic Minor. This means we'll only switch back to C Harmonic Minor for the final bar.

In this example, we'll also use two shapes of F Melodic Minor, so that we cover more of the fretboard.

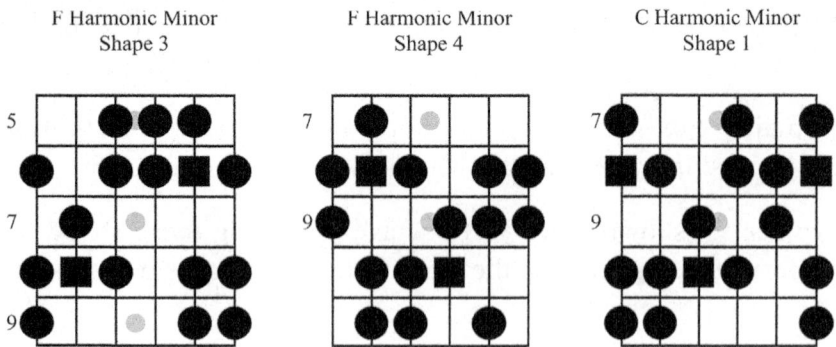

Example 11f

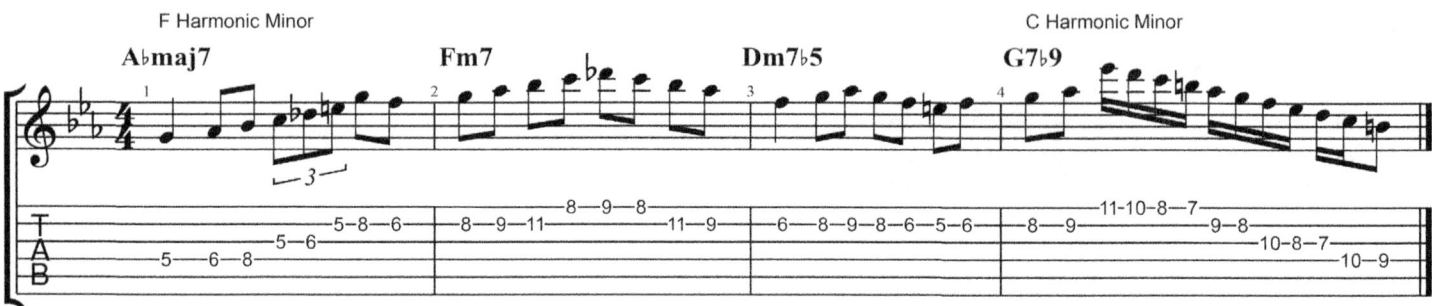

Now it's time to introduce a new idea for this section of the tune. We're going to stick with using F Harmonic Minor over the first three bars, but for bar four we're going to use Ab Melodic Minor (a half step above the G7b9 chord).

This time, rather than play in a single fretboard zone, we'll use the overlapping shapes below, which will extend the range of our line.

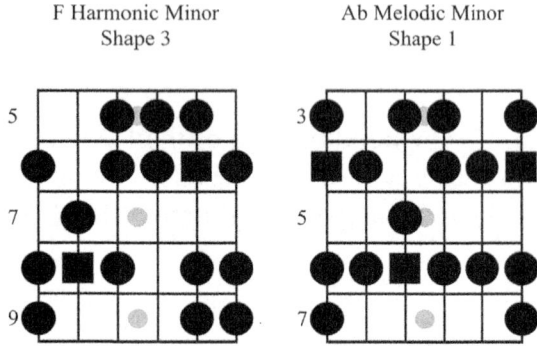

Example 11g

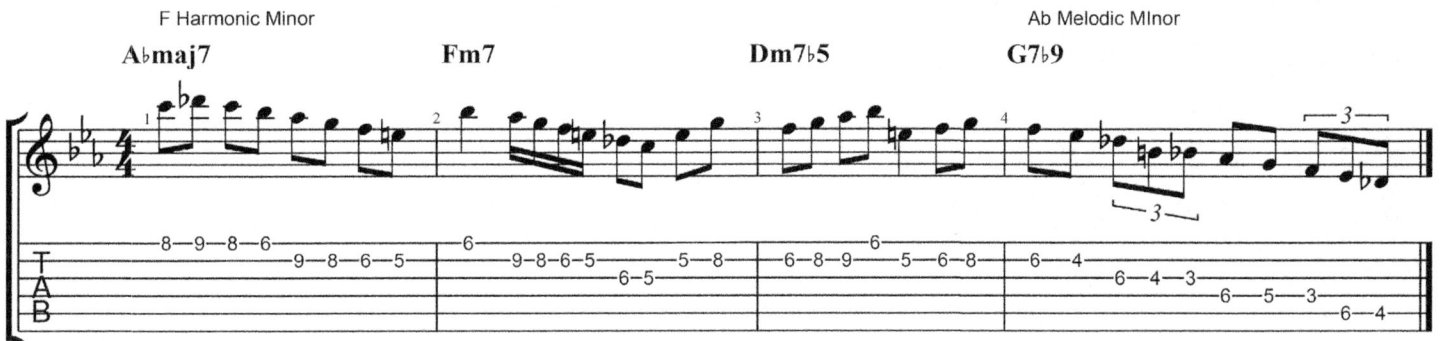

For a spicier option, you'll recall that we can also use Bb Melodic Minor over the G7b9 chord (the melodic minor a minor 3rd above the root of a dominant chord from Chapter Ten).

To create this line, I looked at the whole set of F Harmonic Minor shapes and picked out small triad shapes. The scale notes on the top string provide anchor points to root these little ideas as they climb the neck.

Example 11h

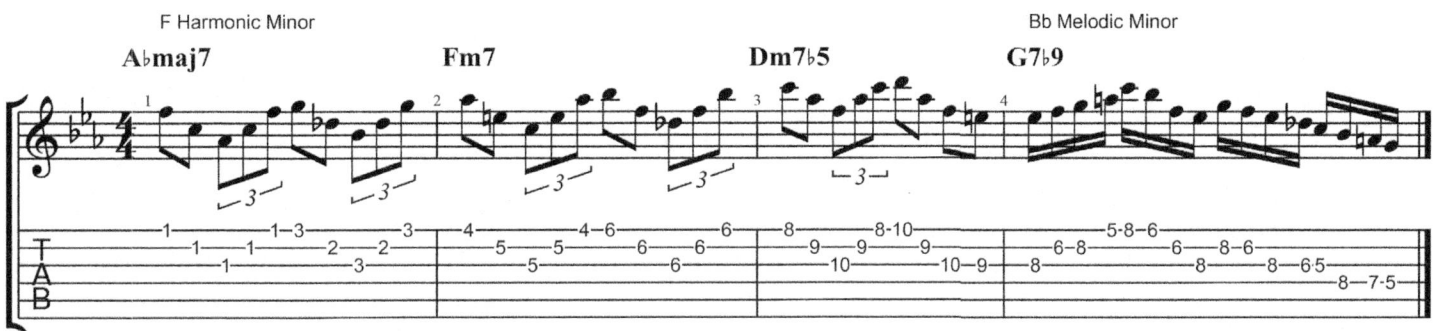

Bars 9-12

Moving on, let's look at bars 9-12 of the tune. Here, the changes are:

| Cm7 | Dm7b5 G7b9 | Cm7 | F7 |

We'll introduce another new idea here and play the G Harmonic Minor scale over Cm7 in bar one. (This is the harmonic minor a 5th above a minor 7 chord substitution we looked at in Chapter Five).

Then we'll move down a whole step to play F Harmonic Minor over Dm7b5 – G7b9 (harmonic minor a minor 3rd above the ii chord).

Over the Cm7 – F7 change, we'll revert to the Bb Major scale to give us a cool Dorian mode sound.

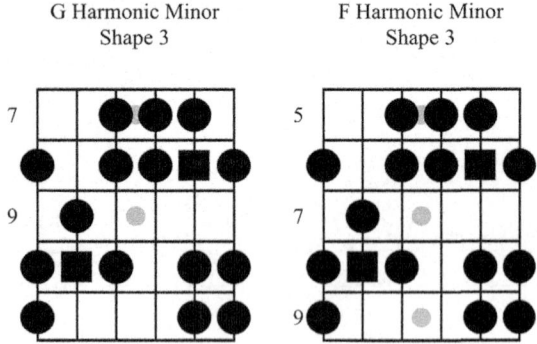

Example 11i

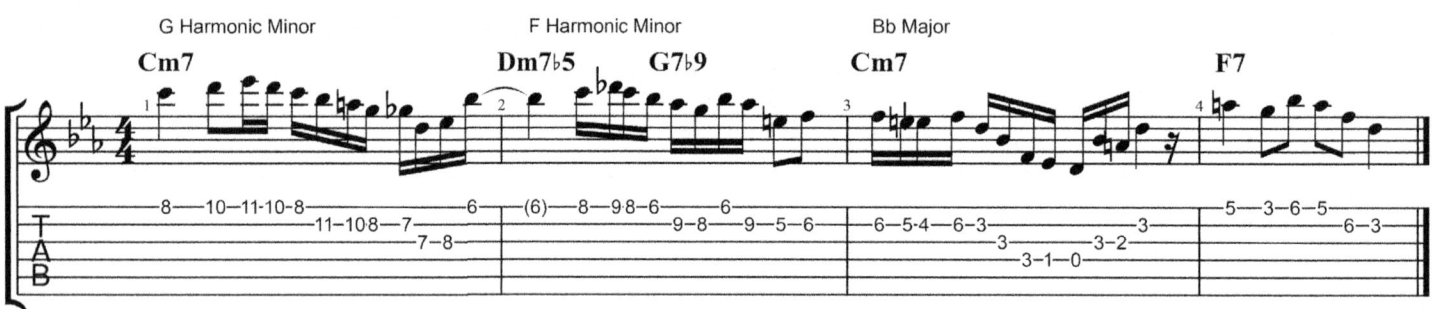

Let's change things up again, this time by playing G Harmonic Minor in bar one, moving to inside sounding arpeggios in bar two, then playing G Harmonic Minor again in bars 3-4.

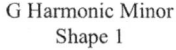
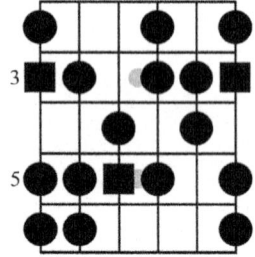

Example 11j

Bars 13-16

The next section of the tune has the following chord changes:

| Abmaj7 | F7 | Fm7b5 | Bb7 |

On some charts you'll see bar three written as Abm6. Don't be confused by this, Fm7b5 and Abm6 contain identical notes, so you could play either chord, but Fm7b5 makes more sense as it creates a ii V movement.

Over bars 1-2 we're going to play the straight Eb Major scale, then move into Eb Harmonic Minor for bars 3-4. Fm7b5 and Bb7 both belong to the harmonized Eb Harmonic Minor scale. Moving between Eb major and Eb minor produces a lovely sound here and is an intuitive movement on guitar. (This is the direct use of the harmonic minor scale in a minor ii V i that we looked at in Chapter Two).

Example 11k

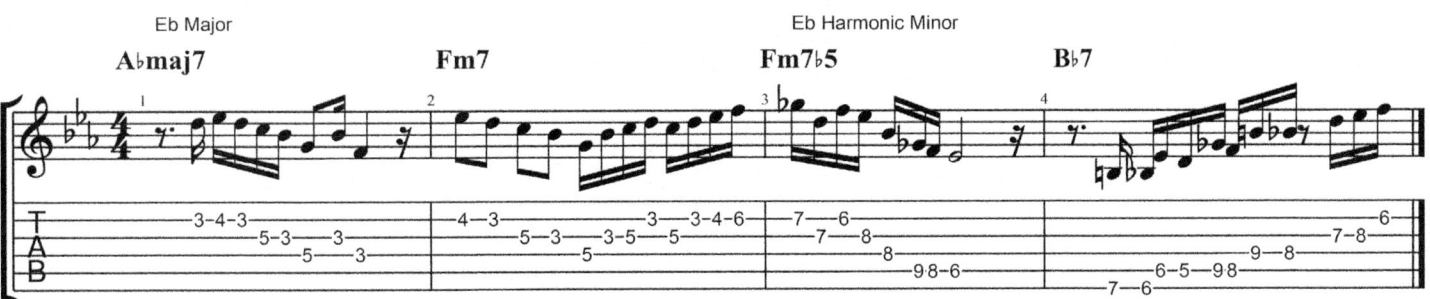

Although we can't do this idea justice here due to space, the major-to-minor approach is a great one to practice because it can easily be achieved with small movements on guitar but has a big harmonic impact.

Let's move things along and try a different approach over these chords. This time we'll use the F Harmonic Minor scale over Abmaj7 – Fm7, and Eb Harmonic Minor again over Fm7b5 – Bb7. This substitution idea introduces a nice, whole step movement between the scale patterns.

The use of the F Harmonic Minor scale here is the "relative minor" substitution we looked at in Chapter Eight, where we played the harmonic minor over a major 7 chord. I.e., F Minor is the relative minor key to Ab Major. (Remember, that's just a quick way of remembering it – I'm not saying F Harmonic Minor is the relative minor key to Ab Major!)

Let's hear how it sounds.

Example 11l

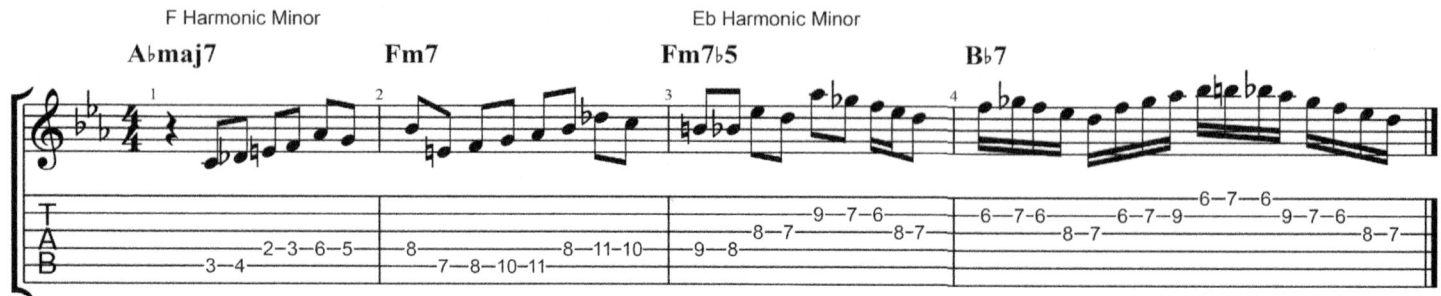

Bars 17-20

There are no substitutions used in this next section, but just for fun, here's Eb Lydian played over this part of the tune to introduce a more modern spin on the harmony. (We need to be careful with the Fm7 chord though, as that's an F7 in Eb Lydian).

Example 11m

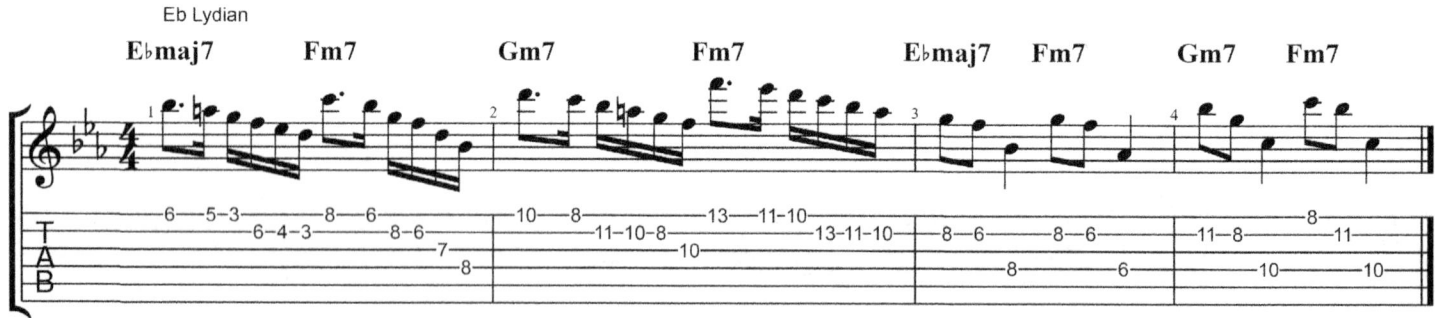

Here's another take on the same theme.

Example 11n

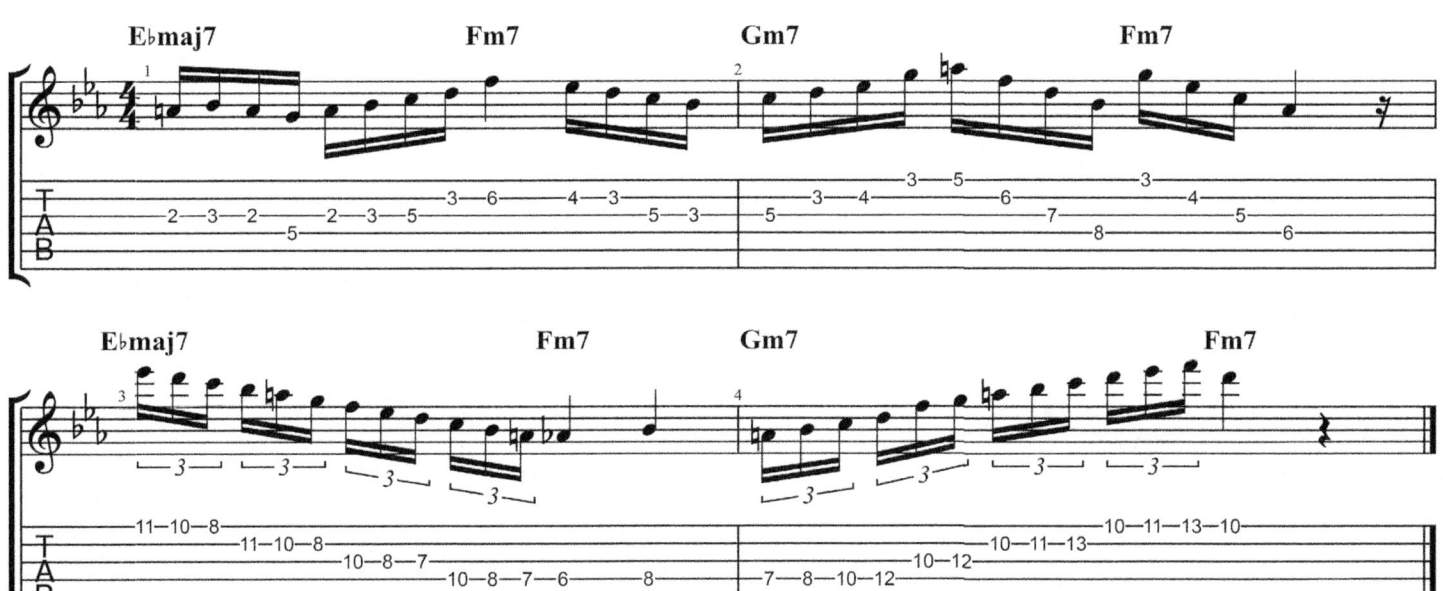

Bars 21-24

In bars 21-24 there are a few more chord changes to navigate than in previous sections. Here, we could say that the point of the progression is to move the focus away from Eb Major (bars 17-20), back to the melancholy C Minor feel. The chord changes are:

| Ebmaj7 G7 | Cm Bm Bbm Eb9 | Abmaj7 | Dm7b5 G7b9 |

Our strategy for employing minor scales here will be to stick to arpeggio ideas for bars 1-2, then use the F Melodic Minor scale over the Abmaj7 chord, and Ab Melodic Minor for the Dm7b5 to G7b9 change.

Example 11o

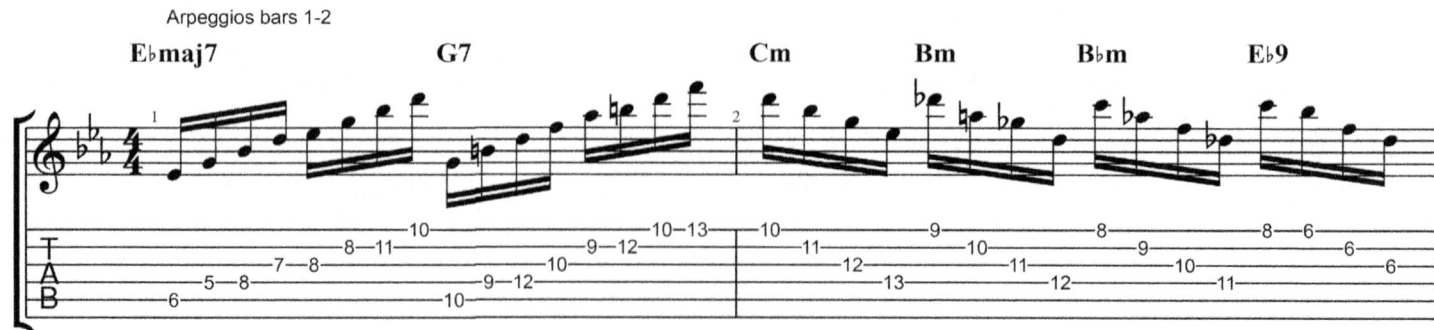

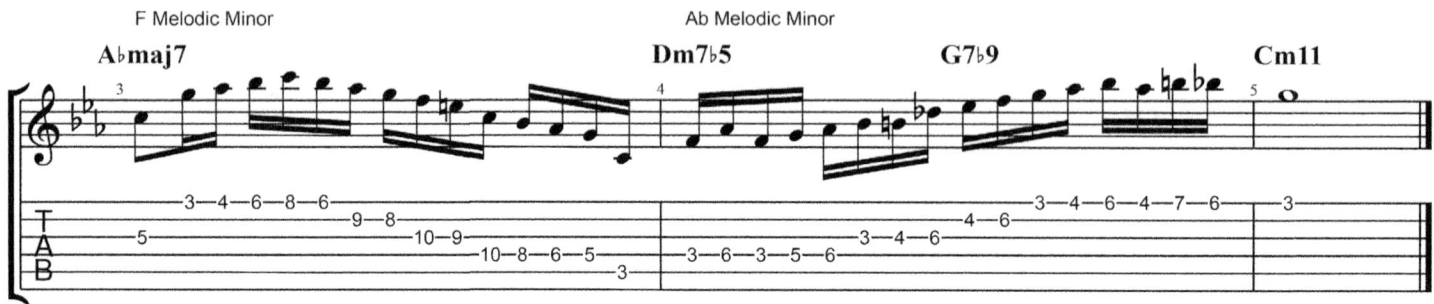

Here's an alternative approach, using the same strategy.

Example 11p

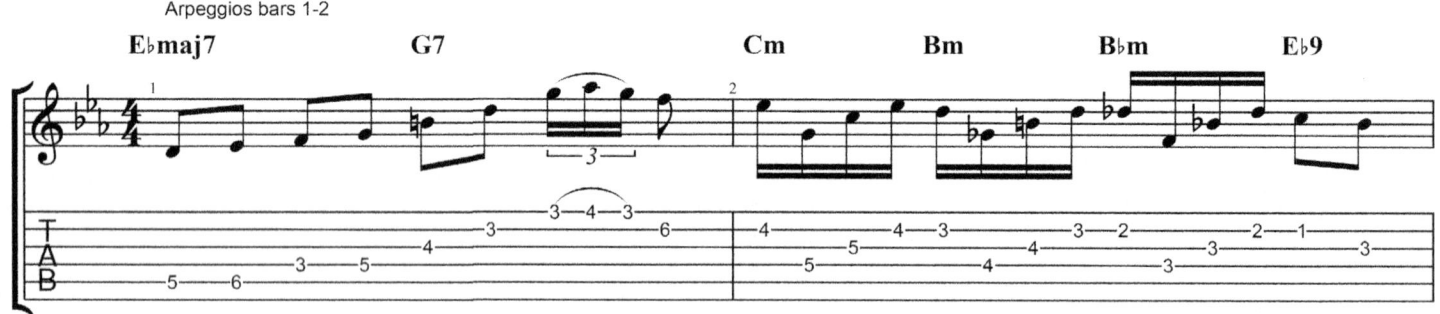

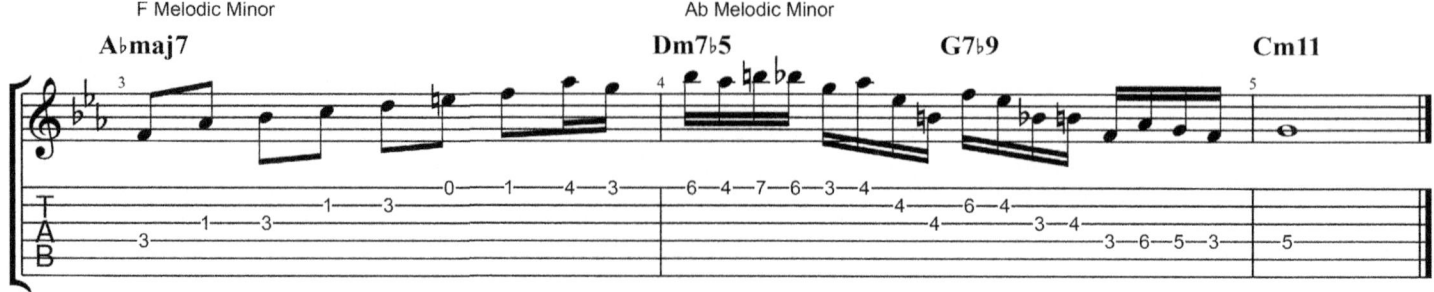

Bars 25-28

The last section of the tune is twelve bars long and similar to the A section but changes up the chords slightly in the final eight bars. Here's one way of playing over that whole twelve-bar section. The substitutions being used are indicated in the TAB. We're going to throw the kitchen sink at this one! It's written in the form of a continuous 1/8th note etude.

Example 11q

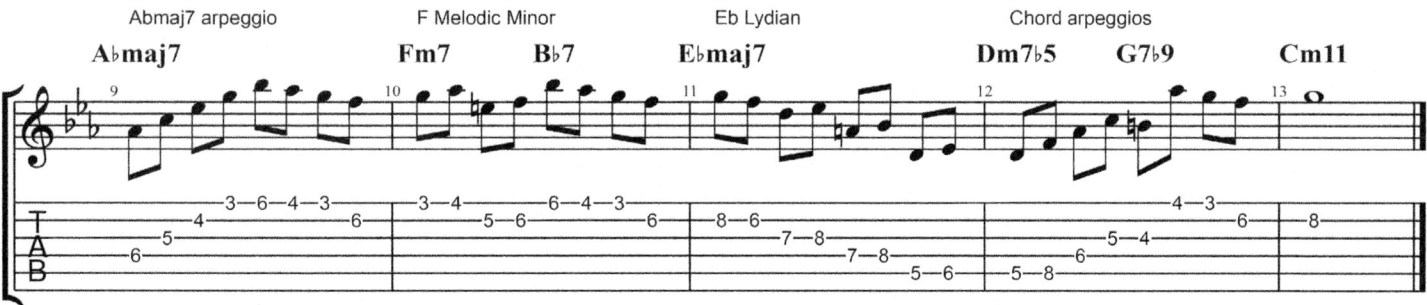

We've now played through the entire (unusual for a standard) 36-bar form of *My Funny Valentine* and looked at an array of substitution options we can use to elevate our melodic ideas above the mundane.

As a next step, I recommend that you make a list of all the ideas used in this chapter and pick just one to work with. Write out the relevant scale shapes for the concept, then work with that idea, soloing over the whole tune. Have several passes at it and play the substitution in a few zones of the fretboard. Get really comfortable with it before you move on.

Then try another, and another… then work on combining ideas. This should keep you busy for a while, but it will be a creative and, I hope, rewarding musical journey.

To get you started, here is one final example. It's a solo over the A section of the tune. Apart from the opening lick, which uses C Harmonic Minor, I've only used *one* substitution idea here – playing the melodic minor scale a half step above the root note of a dominant 7 chord. Whenever the Dm7b5 to G7b9 change occurs, I'm playing Ab Melodic Minor over *both* chords. Apart from that, I'm using regular arpeggio and scale ideas to create the melodic ideas.

If I continued, next I might play F Melodic Minor every time that ii V change occurs (the melodic minor a minor 3rd above a minor chord), but I'll leave you to experiment with that yourself!

Example 11r

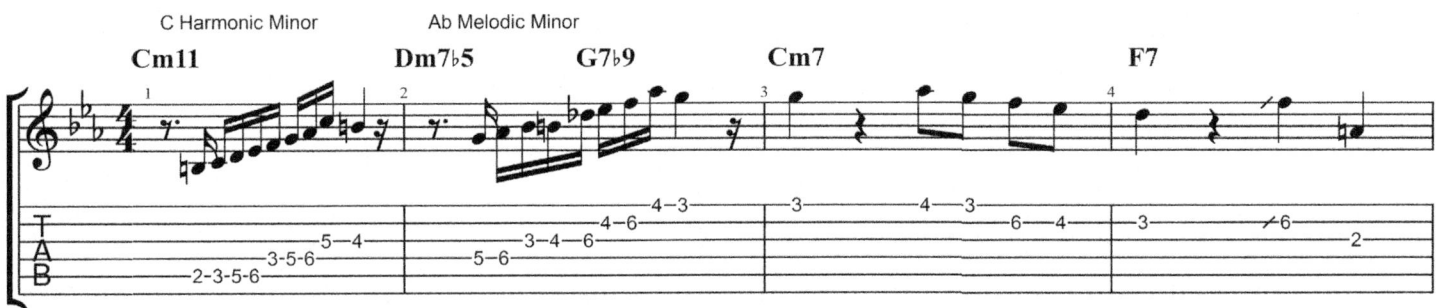
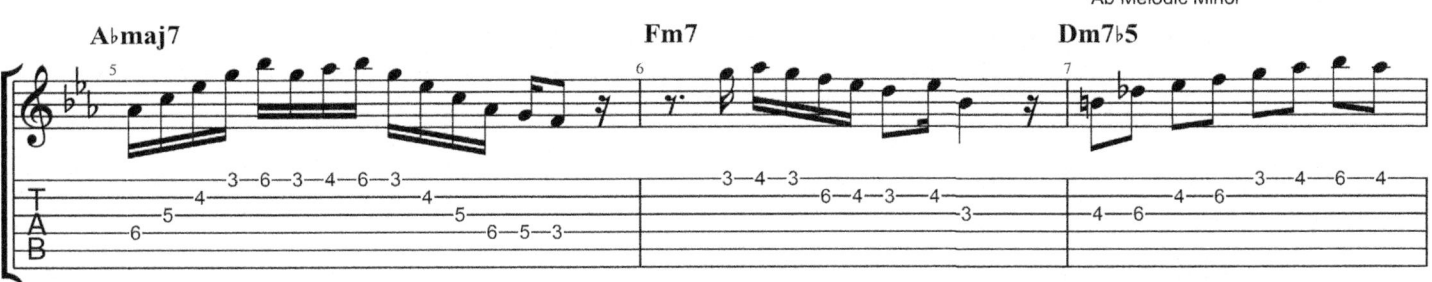
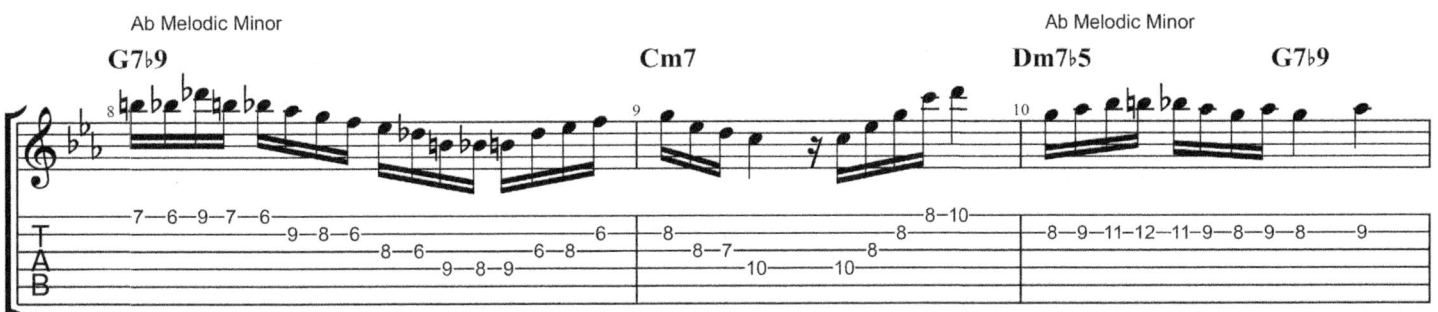
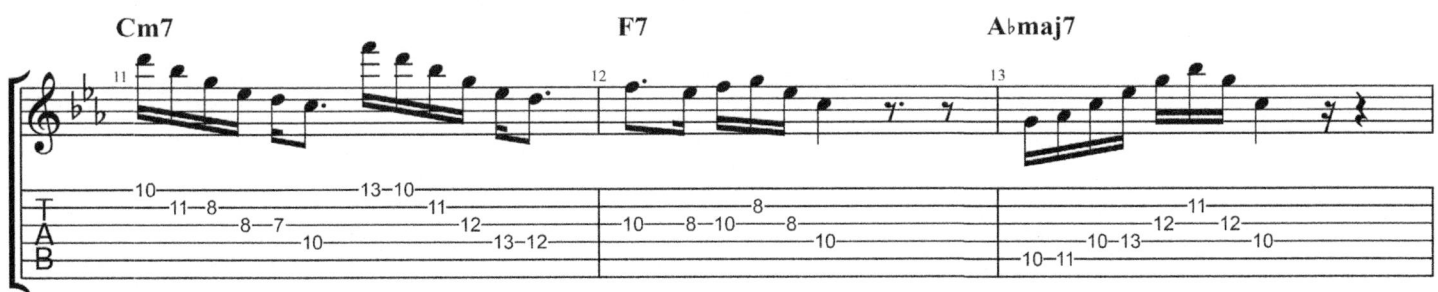
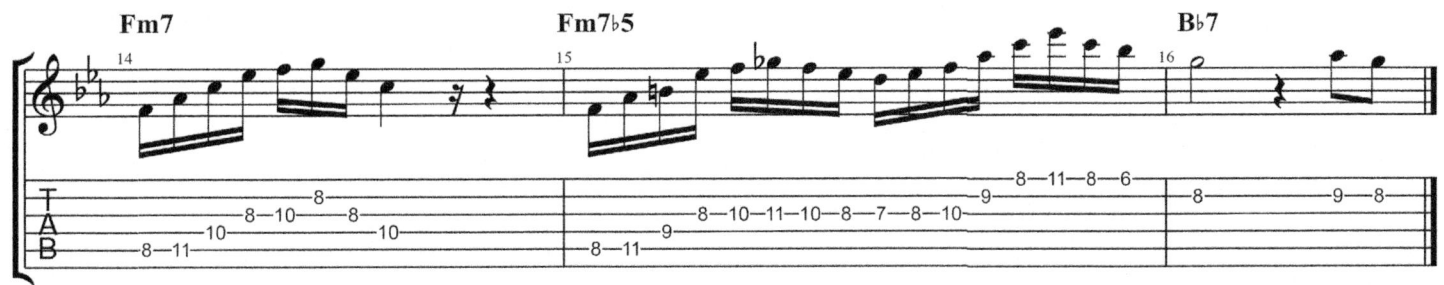

Conclusion

To take these ideas forward, I recommend the following approach to practicing them.

- Practice writing some continuous 1/8th note etudes over the major and minor ii V I backing tracks provided in the audio download, limiting yourself to one substitution idea at a time

- Take a tune you know really well and practice improvising over it, introducing one substitution idea at a time. When you're confident, introduce a second idea

- Write out a soloing scheme, similar to the examples in this chapter, that shows the chord changes and indicates where you intend to use the substitute scale ideas

- Improvise and work out some smooth transition points that will allow you to move in and out of substitute scales in musically pleasing ways. Look for half step movements or whole step movements on the same string

- Don't be afraid to experiment and play some wrong notes. It's all part of refining and developing your style

Above all, have fun and keep listening to the players you love. See if you can hear when these ideas crop up in their playing.

Printed in Great Britain
by Amazon